WE ARE
ALL BLUE

WE ARE ALL BLUE

Two plays by Donald Molosi

Blue, Black and White

&

Motswana: Africa, Dream Again

With a foreword by President Quett Masire

THE MANTLE

New York

The two plays contained in this collection, *Blue, Black and White* and *Motswana: Africa, Dream Again,* are also separately published.

This book was set in Gill Sans MT and Palatino Linotype.

Cover art by Moses Maaramele of Gaborone, Botswana.

Cover design by Tijana Cvetkovic:
(tijanacvetkovic.weebly.com).

THE MANTLE
21-33 36th St.
Queens, NY 11105
mantlebooks.com | @TheMantle

To Omar Sangare, my acting and writing mentor, who is always there—
Dziękuję Ci bardzo.

To Shaun Randol, thank you for believing in my work's value—
ke lebogile, ruri.

CONTENTS

FOREWORD

Donald Molosi's play, *Blue, Black and White* is the first-ever play published about the lives of Sir Seretse and Lady Ruth Khama. Both Sir Seretse and Lady Khama were my close friends in pre-independence times (before 1966), and later during Sir Seretse's tenure as the inaugural President of the Republic of Botswana and I as the inaugural Vice President, until his early death in 1980.

Being one of the world's leading authorities on the epic love story of Sir Seretse and Lady Khama's interracial marriage, Molosi's account of this history is itself an archive of national memory. It therefore gives me great pleasure to say that I was one of the first people to watch the theatrical production of *Blue, Black and White* when it came to Botswana in 2012 and left the nation prideful and in awe.

Apart from the rigorous academic research that Mr. Molosi conducted on three continents for *Blue, Black and White*, he also approached Sir Seretse's friends and contemporaries such as myself for anecdotes. I remember in 2010 Mr. Molosi asked me if I had any humorous memories of my time with Sir Seretse. Below is an excerpt from one of my emails to Mr. Molosi in response:

> *I remember him [Sir Seretse Khama] putting me on the spot in 1962 at our first party conference. I apologized to the conference that I had unfortunately left a copy of congratulations from the Swedish Democratic Party in my other jacket. I was standing and he looked up at me cynically and said, "Do you have another jacket?" The whole conference went roaring with laughter.*

The tenacity that Molosi displays in his excavation and re-imagination of our past must be commended, and it is my hope that he will continue to capture and preserve our stories for coming generations. For instance, in *Motswana: Africa, Dream Again* Molosi captures his generation of Batswana's questions and concerns about self-identity. Never before have we seen a play that meditates on the notion of Motswana in such depth and with such careful nuance.

We Are All Blue comes at an opportune time when Botswana marks 50 years of independence. The volume also comes at the same time as the worldwide screenings of Molosi's own performance opposite Hollywood heavyweights in *A United Kingdom*, a high profile biographical film about Sir Seretse and Lady Khama.

It is especially heartening for my generation of Batswana leaders to note that a young Motswana has chosen to use his God-given talents to honor and document the stories that my generation lived. It is my sincere hope that this necessary book travels far and wide!

—His Excellency Sir Quett Ketumile Joni Masire
Former President of the Republic of Botswana
Gaborone, Botswana
October, 2015

BLUE, BLACK AND WHITE

PRODUCTION HISTORY

Blue, Black and White (*BBW*) was first written and performed in 2008 as a solo play by Donald Molosi. At that time it was titled *Seretse Khama: Blue, Black and White.*

In 2010, Molosi performed *BBW* as a solo at Theatre de Montparnasse in Paris.

In 2011, the show made its off-Broadway premiere in New York City—with Molosi in the title role—at the United Solo Festival, where it won the Best Solo Award. Later in 2011, Molosi performed *BBW* at the University of California, Santa Barbara. That same year, President Ma of Taiwan requested *BBW* to be part of Taiwan's 100 year celebration as a republic. It was performed in Miaoli City and Taipei, with Molosi as the guest artist of the country.

In 2012, *BBW* made its Botswana premiere with Mophato Dance Theater as Molosi's supporting act. Attendees included all four of Sir Seretse Khama's children, his grandchildren, and daughters-in-law. Former President Quett Masire and other dignitaries were also in attendance. With that tour, the show became the longest-running solo play in Botswana's history. Also in 2012, *BBW* headlined the Bucknell Black Arts Festival in Pennsylvania and was performed at Lake Forest College in Illinois.

In early 2013, Molosi released the ensemble version of *BBW* for a performance by The Maitisong Theatre Company when it headlined the Maitisong Festival in Botswana that year.

In 2014, *BBW* toured Brazil, with its premier in Brasilia. The play headlined the Botswana Day celebrations hosted by the Botswana Embassy.

In May 2015, *BBW* premiered in South Africa at the historic Tigerkloof Educational Institution in Vryburg. Also in 2015, *BBW* premiered in Kenya at Nairobi University and premiered in Belgium at Brussels' historic Theatre du Vaudeville.

In April 2016 *BBW* headlines the inaugural Folk Tale Theatre Festival in Botswana.

AWARDS

In 2008, *Blue, Black and White* won the Best Actor Award at the Dialogue One Festival in Massachusetts.

In 2011, the show made its off-Broadway premiere in New York City—with Molosi in the title role—at the United Solo Festival, where it won the Best Solo Award.

In 2013, the ensemble version of *BBW* won the Dilling Yang Prize for Excellence in Playwriting from the University of California Santa Barbara.

BBW is the longest-ever running one-man-show in Botswana, the first play ever about Botswana to be staged off-Broadway, and the first Botswana play to win major theatre awards.

PLAYWRIGHT'S NOTE

Who is to say that dreams are any less true than the history that we learn in schools? History—after all—like dreams and memory, is a fictitious assemblage of facts to construct a specific narrative. The fictitiousness of the histories that we learn in schools the world over is no more evident than in the same histories' paucity of humanist stories about Africans. In this global pretense, the only African stories that deserve telling are the ones where the African's full humanity is apparently subverted by war, servitude, backwardness, etc. This general absence of the African's agency in history is the artificial gap in global history that I seek to trouble: what about the African stories of glamour and humor and feminism? What about the love stories that occur in dialectical opposition to their African setting?

When I began to transcribe my dreams about Sir Seretse Khama in 2007, I ended up with enough material to create a one-man play which I called *Blue, Black and White*. I subsequently performed it off-Broadway under the mentorship of Polish director Omar Sangare. In 2010, I began to rigorously research the facts about the story of Sir Seretse and Lady Khama. That investigation spawned a longer version of the piece. What I present in this book is a two-act ensemble play based on fact but with a few anachronisms (like the inclusion of Miriam Makeba's music).

The few anachronisms are based on my own dreams of that specific moment in history; to what extent can the present gaze at the past without the present projecting itself onto the past? What insights about history as fiction emerge when we juxtapose academic fact with material from dreams? In Botswana, like in many African settings, dreams are traditionally understood—among other things—as archives of collective human experience that exist in a trans-generational matrix where linear time collapses and daily life is lived in communion with collective ancestors. Our ancestors are biologically dead but spiritually immortal.

By definition, humanity is shared and so it cannot be truly practiced in isolation from other members of the so-called "global village." Thus, I posit in *Blue, Black and White* that our lack of knowledge of each other's stories as global villagers is a site of post-colonial trauma. I also believe that although we are all blue—severed from our own history—acquainting ourselves with the stories of those different from ourselves alleviates that same trauma.

Blue, Black and White is the first play published about the interracial marriage of Sir Seretse and Lady Ruth Khama. It is my hope that there will be many more re-imaginations of this story by other storytellers.

***

I dedicate this play to the memory of Sir Seretse and Lady Ruth Khama, and to my grandmother Kelebjwang Molosi in this her 94th year of life. And, as always, to my mother Gosego Molosi.

—Donald Molosi
Gaborone, Botswana
October, 2015

CAST OF CHARACTERS

The whole ensemble comprises of three men and three women. No two characters are the same. Lefika, Aishwarya, Tuelo, Jung-Hwa, Frank, and Ajani are students who also become other characters in the flashback scenes.

LEFIKA (meaning "Refuge" in Setswana): Lefika is an 11-year-old introverted Motswana (Mongwato) boy with a fantastic talent for performance. His grades in the classroom, however, are average. The same actor also plays Villager 1 and Seretse Khama.

AISHWARYA (meaning "Prosperity" in Hindi): Aishwarya is a nine-year-old Indian-Motswana girl. She is confident and from a wealthy family. Her hair is always in a long braid down her back. The same actress also plays Villager 2, Bongani, and Ruth's mother.

TUELO (meaning "Reparation" in Setswana): Tuelo is a 10-year-old Motswana (Moyei) boy. He is loud-spoken, fidgety, and quick to smile. He has a thick Yei accent. The same actor also plays Villager 3, and Uncle Tshekedi.

JUNG-HWA (meaning "Righteous" in Korean): Jung-Hwa is an 11-year-old Korean girl. She is studious and over-confident. She wears thick glasses and speaks with a clipped British accent typical of those who have attended private school before. The same actress also plays Villager 4, President Masire, and Sipho.

TEACHER: She is 25 years old and has just graduated from the Serowe Teacher Training College. She is overly strict because she is anxious about students getting too casual with her. The same actress also plays Ruth.

AJANI (meaning "Of Noble Birth" in Yoruba): Ajani was born in Botswana to Nigerian parents. She is 12 years old and downplays her Nigerian background, as it is usually a source of xenophobic ridicule. The same actor plays Daniel Malan,

Poet, Ayanda, and BBC Announcer.

FRANK: Frank is a 10-year-old blonde British boy. He is outspoken, stubborn, and intelligent. He wears braces on his teeth. The same actor plays Villager 5 and Ruth's father.

MILDRED: Mildred is 11 years old and she was born to a white British mother and a black British father. Her hair is curly and she wears a lot of bangles around her wrists. The same actress plays Ian Smith.

NOTES ON SET DESIGN AND COSTUMES

The action takes place during history class in a typical classroom in a Botswana public school. The enthusiastic, newly graduated young teacher treats her students to a special history lesson that does not exist in their textbooks. She, too, learns a great deal. During the lesson, flashbacks are staged as a story-telling device and in these moments new scenes are presented in different settings.

As far as costumes go, anything minimal but effective will do for quick changes. Students must wear uniforms, over which they wear costumes of other characters in flashbacks. The schoolboy uniforms include khaki shorts and white shirts with yellow neckties, black socks, and black shoes. The girls' uniforms are khaki skirts and white blouses with yellow woolen waist-ties.

All scenes are named in various languages that are spoken by different people who call Botswana home in the twenty-first century. The titles could be seen as descriptions of Botswana's postcolonial condition. The non-English lines may not be omitted or translated into English in production.

BLUE, BLACK AND WHITE

by
Donald Molosi

Based on the lives of Sir Seretse Khama (1921-1980)
and Lady Ruth Khama (1923-2002),
and the history of a nation.

ACT I

Prologue

Out beyond ideas of wrongdoing and right doing there is a field. I'll meet you there. When the soul lies down in that grass, the world is too full to talk about. — *Rumi*

قوشعم روا قشاع
("Lover and Beloved" in Urdu)

Present day is July 2002. A multiracial group of students enters and performs a folktale as the villagers of Serowe, perhaps accompanied by live guitar music. The students are also putting together the set and putting on costume as they tell the story.

This folktale is the theme to the class's commemoration of Sir Seretse Khama Week, especially today (July 1) being Sir Seretse Khama Day. The class is also honoring Sir Seretse's wife, Lady Ruth, who passed away two months prior to July 1, 2002.

ALL VILLAGERS: We begin this Sir Seretse Khama Week with the folktale that is our theme. The folktale is about a boy who brought his father back from the dead.

VILLAGER 1: It is said that there was once a boy who was living in a land far away from his *kgota*, his home. His father died while the boy was very young, so he did not know his father.

VILLAGER 2: When the boy was growing up and became aware that he did not have a father, he asked his mother.

ALL VILLAGERS: Mother, where is my father?

VILLAGER 3: And his mother replied—

ALL VILLAGERS: Your father is dead, my son. His name was Ngwedi, which means "the moon."

VILLAGER 4: His mother had also since died. *Hei!*

VILLAGER 1: Now that the boy was growing older, he found himself wondering a lot about his father.

VILLAGER 4: People around him were treating the boy badly and beat him for no reason. He wanted his father's protection.

VILLAGER 3: He wondered and wondered about his father and wanted desperately to see him. He wondered for days and weeks and months.

VILLAGER 2: One day he decided to yoke the donkeys to the wagon and set off for his father's family dwelling place, his father's *kgota*.

VILLAGER 1: Since his father's name was Ngwedi, the *kgota* was also called Ngwedi, because he had been its headman when he was alive.

VILLAGER 2: It was evening when the boy left for his father's *kgota* and the clouds were gathering over the moon. On the way he met a woman and sang out to her—

ALL VILLAGERS: Take heed, those who delay me! Where is Ngwedi's *kgota*? Listen to what I ask, for the clouds are where the moon was. Don't delay me.

VILLAGER 1: The woman said—

ALL VILLAGERS: Stay on this road, *ngwanaka*. You will meet some people going there. Ask them.

VILLAGER 3: Stay on this road. You will meet some people going there. Ask them.

VILLAGER 1: The boy continued his journey. On the way he met a man and he sang—

ALL VILLAGERS: Take heed, those who delay me! Where is Ngwedi's *kgota*? Listen to what I ask, for the clouds are where the moon was. Don't delay me.

VILLAGER 2: The old woman pointed to a place and said—

ALL VILLAGERS: That is the *kgota* you want over there, *ngwana-ka*. Turn off the gravel road, walk a little bit and you will get to it.

VILLAGER 3: That is the *kgota* you want over there. Turn off the gravel road, walk a little bit and you will get to it.

VILLAGER 2: When the boy reached the *kgota*, he said to the people there—

LEFIKA: I am Morwangwedi, the son of Ngwedi. I want black sheep and white oxen; kill them for me. I am looking for the place where my father was buried.

VILLAGER 4: And so the people of the *kgota* took him to the kraal and showed him his father's grave. The boy dug out his father's bones and fastened them together. When he had done this, he took the meat of the sheep and oxen and put it on the bones. Then the boy began to sing—

LEFIKA: Take heed, those who delay me! Where is Ngwedi's shirt? Listen to what I ask, for the clouds are where the moon was. Don't delay me.

(As each item of clothing is mentioned, the villagers pull it out of their baskets and dress Lefika in it. Every time he puts on a new item of clothing he transforms more into Sir Seretse Khama. Lefika is isolated from the rest of the ensemble. Soft, ethereal guitar music plays.)

VILLAGER 3: So the people of the *kgota* gave him his father's shirt, and he put it on top of the meat of oxen and sheep, which was fastened to the bones.

VILLAGER 2: Then the boy asked for his father's trousers in the same way.

VILLAGER 1: And his shoes.

VILLAGER 2: All the time urging them to hurry because the clouds were covering the moon.

VILLAGER 4: When the flesh was clothed, his father came to life! The boy yoked the donkeys, took his father, and set off back to where the boy had been living as an orphan. And when he arrived with his father, the people treated the boy like a king.

ALL VILLAGERS: They did not treat him badly like before, because now he had his father to protect him.

(There is much jubilation and ululation. Lefika, one of the students has been transformed by the costume into Sir Seretse Khama. He poses as a statue of Sir Seretse and then melts out of the pose to deliver the following version of one of Sir Seretse's speeches. Ensemble gathers around him and uses their bodies and configuration to establish a radio station studio and a microphone that Sir Seretse is speaking into. No music.)

LEFIKA: *(Putting on his glasses.)* Bagaetsho, we must write our history books to prove that we did have a past, and that this is a past that is just as worth writing and learning about as any other. My fellow Batswana, we must excavate our history, dress it up in pride, intelligence, and foresight so that it may indeed come alive in our consciousness today.

(Lights fade and the rest of the speech is done in the fade-out to imply evanescent memory, or a glimpse.)

We must connect the present to the past so that the future may be secured. Because the past can disappear.

Scene 1
Tortura
("Torture" in Spanish)

Teacher enters and she is happy with the students' presentation. She wears oversized reading glasses. She is in her mid-twenties and there is a bossy air about her.

TEACHER: Memorized just like a tape recorder. Well done to you, class! Lefika, go ahead and put away the costume. Well done. This Sir Seretse Khama Day is going to be superb, isn't it? Well done, everyone.

ALL STUDENTS: Thank you, Teacher.

TEACHER: Tuelo! Tell us the moral of the folktale.

TUELO: The moral of de story is dat when we know our history we put de smile on de face of ancestor and he come alive!

TEACHER: *Ehee!* That is the exact theme of the week. Keep it up. Now, everyone, let us begin today's special lesson.

(Students put away the bits of costume used for the skit. Two students go offstage and bring an easel. Another two bring a blackboard. There is much chit-chat and giggling as the students swiftly prepare for the lesson. Students then sit facing upstage. Teacher pulls out a stick from her bag and begins to swing it casually. This is only her second term teaching, having just graduated from Teachers College. Perhaps she is too eager.)

TEACHER: Good morning, children.

(All students stand to show respect.)

ALL STUDENTS: Good morning, Teacher!

TEACHER: Children, how are you?

ALL STUDENTS: We are fine, Teacher. Thank you.

TEACHER: Yes. Very well. You may sit down.

(Students sit.)

Who can tell the class what the date is today?

(Several students raise their hands. Teacher picks Lefika, who does not

have his hand raised. As a rule, students stand up whenever they are addressing the teacher and then they sit down again when they are finished.)

Yes, Lefika. Why don't you tell us what the date is today?

LEFIKA: The... the day. The date. Today the date—

TEACHER: *(She hits him hard with the stick and he is squirming and making sounds of pain.)* Ah, *waitse wena!* In class you stammer. And yet when we do sketches you are fine. When are you ever going to stop being such a dunderhead? How many times have you repeated grade seven? *Ija.*

(She points to Jung-Hwa, Frank, and Aishwarya as she mentions them below.)

Look at your mates. Jung-Hwa and Frank and Aishwarya are writing the Primary School Leaving Examinations next term and *wena*, not even a simple date can you say!

Hmm. You children think Primary School is hard? Heh! Wait until you get to the teachers' training college—you will shit yourselves from hard work.

(She moves on to another student who has her hand raised.)

Yes, Aishwarya!

AISHWARYA: Today is Monday, July 1, 2002.

TEACHER: Excellent!

(Teacher begins to write date on the blackboard but her piece of chalk breaks. She checks the chalk box for more and finds it empty. She then calls out to one of the students to go fetch more chalk.)

Hmm... I know some of you naughty children steal my chalk. The day I catch the chalk thief! Hmm... *(Calling out to Lefika.)* Lefika! Go next door and ask the teacher there for colored chalk.

LEFIKA: Ye-ye...yes, Teacher.

(Lefika gets up. He is moving slowly and has a general sleepiness about him.)

TEACHER: *(Laughing and teasing Lefika.)* The way this boy walks around with his spirit under his feet!

(She shakes her head and curls her lips.) I don't even know how he does so well in sketches!

(She then turns to the class.) Class, who can tell us what history is?

(Aishwarya enthusiastically raises her hand.)

Yes, Aishwarya!

AISHWARYA: History is the study of the past.

TEACHER: Superb. Repeat, class!

ALL STUDENTS: History is the study of the past.

TEACHER: Agaaaaain!

ALL STUDENTS: History is the study of the past.

TEACHER: Terrific. We are going to learn more about the first president of Botswana because today is his day. Tell me again, who was the first president of Botswana?

(Students raise hands.)

Yes, Mildred!

(Lefika ambles in with chalk and hands it to the teacher before sitting down.)

MILDRED: The first president of Botswana was Sir Seretse Khama.

TEACHER: Super! Date of birth and date of death?

JUNG-HWA: *(Frantically trying to get chosen to answer. Loudly.)* Me, teacher! Me teacher meteachermeteach —

TEACHER: Hey, Jung-Hwa, why are you scattering your voice like that? Are you in a fish market or a classroom?

(Teacher curls her lip in disapproval.) Hmm... Yes, you cantankerous girl. What is the answer?

JUNG-HWA: Sir Seretse Khama was born on the first of July, 1921 and died on the thirteenth of July, 1980.

TEACHER: Well done!

(Pause.)

It is very important for you all to learn history because why? Because you are the young generation and you must dig up the history of Botswana. Are you with me?

ALL STUDENTS: Yes, Teacher.

TEACHER: Now you all know the folktale of Morwangwedi, right?

ALL STUDENTS: Yes, Teacher.

TEACHER: Today we are going to be like that boy in the folktale, okay?

ALL STUDENTS: Yes, Teacher.

TEACHER: When you know your history, you put a smile on the face of our ancestors. I say we must read. We must revise.

(Brief pause.) Sir Seretse Khama was the Founding Father. Do you follow?

ALL STUDENTS: Yes, Teacher.

FRANK: Teacher, why are we making it sound like he is the only one? My father says that there were also other people who helped found the Republic. Edison Masisi. Motsamai Mpho—

TEACHER: *(Interrupting him.) Hei!* There was only one president!

(Pause.)

Class, does Sir Seretse Khama deserve to be honored?

ALL STUDENTS: Yes, Teacher.

TEACHER: Does his life story deserve to be in your textbooks?

ALL STUDENTS: Yes, Teacher.

TEACHER: Is his life story in your history textbooks?

ALL STUDENTS: No, Teacher.

(Long pause as Teacher shakes her head. The silence is broken by Frank.)

FRANK: I mean, Teacher, even Nswazwi, King of the Kalangas, is not in our textbook. And he is also important.

TEACHER: *(Shaking her head.)* I am going to ignore you, Frank. Let us hear the questions that you children have about Sir Seretse Khama. But first let me deal with Frank.

(She beats Frank with the stick.)

FRANK: *(After receiving his beating.)* Teacher, you cannot change the fact that other people created this country. Just because they were not Bangwato, doesn't mean we don't talk about them. My father told me!

TEACHER: This new tendency of yours to be rude will make you miserable in this class, Frank. You hear me? Nonsensical boy. What do you know? You are just a child of yesterday.

AISHWARYA: Teacher, I have a question.

TEACHER: *(To Aishwarya.)* And you think you can speak without raising your hand? Anyhow, go on.

AISHWARYA: How did Sir Seretse and Lady Ruth meet?

TEACHER: Well, let us use our imagination.

> *(Excited.)* I will play Lady Ruth. *Kana,* she has always been my role model.

Scene 2
Ditshimologo
("Beginnings" in Setswana)

Nutford House, London. The year is 1947. Ensemble morphs into the characters in this scene. The college students, all of them in their mid-twenties, are from the British colonies. They are gathered in a semi-circle and introducing themselves. The students are from all over the world to give the feel of the Commonwealth. Ensemble plays roles of the foreign students. Teacher plays Ruth and Lefika plays Seretse.

RUTH: Hello, everyone. It is lovely to meet you all. My sister Muriel and I are happy you invited us to your dinner here at Nutford House. We hope we can be part of your home away from your homes. Through the London Missionary Society, of course.

ALL FOREIGN STUDENTS: *(This "Thank You" is not chorused. The students say so in a staggered manner.)* Thank you.

RUTH: Shall we do introductions, everyone? I will begin. I am Ruth, Muriel's sister. I work as a clerk here in London.

STEFAN: My name is Stefan. I'm from Jamaica and I'm here

studying physics at Cambridge University. I come to London often to visit my boooring uncle who lives here, in Lewisham.

(Stefan mock-yawns when he says "boring" and other students laugh.)

RUTH: Welcome, Stefan.

JULIUS: I am Julius from Tanzania and I am at Oxford. I am studying PPE—philosophy, politics, and economics.

GRACE: Your name is not Mwisho?

JULIUS: Haha! I don't use my Swahili name anymore, Grace. Haha.

RUTH: Okay.

GRACE: *Néih hóu.* That means "hello" in Cantonese! I am Grace from Hong Kong. I am happy to be in London and meet you all this weekend. Like Julius, I am at Oxford. My course is medicine.

RUTH: Welcome, Grace.

SERETSE: Hello. I am Seretse. I am from Bechuanaland Protectorate, a place that we who are from there call Botswana. It's next to South Africa. I am at Oxford. Let's see... I hate courses in Greek.

(Everyone laughs.)

I am 27 and I play football. I can kick a ball from Cape Town to Cairo.

(Everyone laughs again.)

I also love jazz. That's all.

RUTH: Seretse, you said?

SERETSE: Yes. My name is Seretse.

RUTH: You enjoy jazz? I like jazz quite a bit myself. Say, who are you listening to lately?

SERETSE: Well, I enjoy American jazz. But there is a new South African artist called Miriam —

RUTH: Makeba! Miriam Makeba. I adore her!

SERETSE: I am surprised you have heard of her.

(Calvin enters late.)

CALVIN: Sorry everyone. I had to call home quickly.

RUTH: Her voice is breathtaking. I had better have heard of her!

(Ruth and Seretse share a laugh.)

STEFAN: What is her name again?

CALVIN: Who?

SERETSE: Miriam Makeba.

(To Ruth.) Who do you listen to?

RUTH: Well, let us see. Louis Armstrong comes to mind. Ella Fitzgerald. Some Motown, it is not jazz exactly but it is also quite good in itself.

SERETSE: Do you like the Ink Spots?

RUTH: That is my favorite band!

CALVIN: *(Awkwardly snaking himself into conversation.)* I have their record. Oh, excuse me, everyone. I had to make a telephone call. My name is Calvin Mwenda. I am from Kenya. I study geography. And yes! I have the Ink Spots record!

SERETSE: Really? You will have to share that with everyone sometime, Calvin.

CALVIN: *(Too enthusiastic.)* Definitely, chap! Good music, there. Haha. By the way everyone, I just got engaged!

ALL FOREIGN STUDENTS: Congratulations!

STEFAN: Where is she from?

CALVIN: Malaysia. It is very difficult for us, this interracial business.

RUTH: I cannot even imagine. Congratulations on the engagement.

(Pause.)

Say, since I have the new Miriam Makeba, how would you like to exchange it for your Ink Spots? A borrowing exchange?

CALVIN: Certainly! I even wish I could hear Miriam Makeba right away. Haha!

SERETSE: *(Theatrically imitating Miriam Makeba in jest.)* Saguquka sathi beka! Saguquka sathi beka!

(Everyone laughs and so does Seretse.)

RUTH: *(Teasing.)* That is my favorite song on the record. Stop taking the mickey out of it!

(Seretse laughs.)

I wish I could make Zulu click sounds like Miriam.

SERETSE: *(Seretse sings the song again being the theatrical jokester and Ruth joins in earnest. There is a lot of laughter.)* Saguquka sathi beka!

RUTH: *Nantsi pata pata!*

GRACE: *(To one of the students.)* She knows the words!

(Seretse gets up and dances a mock Sophiatown dance and Ruth laughingly joins. Everyone is much shyer than these two.)

SERETSE: *Saguquka sathi beka!*

RUTH: *Nantsi pata pata!*

("Pata Pata" by Miriam Makeba begins to play in order to evoke the era and the two dance to a bit of it. Lights fade.)

Scene 3
Etre Orphelins
("To Be Orphans" in French)

Back to the classroom.

AISHWARYA: Teacher, Lefika even looks like a young Sir Seretse Khama.

JUNG-HWA: Yes, he even looks like him! *(Jung-Hwa laughs a brief laugh, amazed.)*

FRANK: Of course he does. They are from the same ethnic group. Might even be related.

TEACHER: *(Clearly ignoring Frank's comment.)* Well done, Lefika. Take seats, everybody. Let us continue the lesson. Class, Sir Seretse Khama was a member of the royal what?

ALL STUDENTS: Family.

TEACHER: Which tribe?

ALL STUDENTS: Bangwato.

AISHWARYA: My father says it is not good to use the word "tribe."

TEACHER: Is he your teacher or am I your teacher? Hmm...These big-mouthed students of today! Anyway, I hope you all memorized the Royal Family tree from last class.

(Teacher waves her stick at Aishwarya.) What are the names of Sir Seretse Khama's children?

AJANI: Jacqueline, Ian, Anthony, and Tshekedi!

TEACHER: *Hei wena!* Did I point at you? Hmm... And who is Sir Seretse Khama's father?

(She points at Aishwarya.)

AISHWARYA: King Sekgoma!

TEACHER: And who is Sekgoma's father?

(Teacher thinks she just posed a tough trick question. She is reveling in self satisfaction when Jung-Hwa raises her hand. She points at Jung-Hwa.)

JUNG-HWA: King Khama the Third.

TEACHER: *(Disappointed that someone knows the answer.)* Yes.

(Smugly.) Also called Khama the Great. Understood, everyone?

ALL STUDENTS: Yes, Teacher.

JUNG-HWA: Is it true that if you look at the sky you can see clouds shaped like Sir Seretse Khama's face?

TUELO: Is it true dat Sir Seretse had a battery in his heart? *Gatwe o ne a na le watch mo pelong!*

AJANI: Teacher, Teacher! Is it true that his white wife did not want to live close to Batswana people in Serowe? Is that why they lived on a hill?

TEACHER: You three are full of jokes. Now tell me, children, how do you think the tribe reacted to the news of a British wife for King Seretse? Use your imagination.

Scene 4
Великое смешение
("Great Confusion" in Russian)

The children transform into villagers of Serowe, doing their chores on the farms. The villagers are discussing the latest news about their King Seretse Khama, who is studying far away from home, in England. Students slowly sing one line of "Bagammangwato Ba Ga Mabiletsa" as they transform into the villagers.

Lyrics:
Sekgoma ka e le ngwana wa monna,
Sekgoma le ene a le e biletsa!

VILLAGER 1: *(Fanning herself.)* Hei mma, this heat!

VILLAGER 2: Hei! *(Pointing in the direction of the tree.)* Yesterday I had to sit under that morula tree by the clinic aaaaaalllll day. The sun was just too merciless.

VILLAGER 1: I hope it will rain tonight. With this cruel heat we are almost dying!

VILLAGER 2: We are almost dying!

(They laugh.)

VILLAGER 3: *Dumelang!* Hmm... Even the sun is behaving strangely, isn't it? The things that are going on in Serowe these days! *Ijo!*

VILLAGER 1: *Ah mma,* what do you mean?

VILLAGER 3: Nothing. It is just that with this new affair things are bound to be peculiar.

VILLAGER 5: Hmm... Things have always been "peculiar" for some of us Kalangas. How about the fact that this very Kingdom of Seretse Khama still treats us like we are inferior? *Mxm!*

VILLAGER 3: *Mma,* do you ever not complain? It is as though you win fat cows for being so bitter!

VILLAGER 5: Trust me, *mma,* I would be quiet if things were fair. A bullfrog never growls when no rain has fallen.

VILLAGER 3: Anyway, I was telling you women that things are upside down.

VILLAGER 2: Are you referring to Kgosi Seretse taking a white bride?

VILLAGER 3: Yes! It is too much! *(Resting her wrists on her waist.)* Will this white woman even know how to make a decent pot of *phaleche*? I tell you, the things that are going on these days.

VILLAGER 1: They say Kgosi Seretse is already planning his trip back to discuss this matter with us here in Serowe.

VILLAGER 2: Will that not just pour water onto simmering fat?

VILLAGER 3: I say, will this white woman even know how to tie a proper tukwi around her head? *Hei!* The things we see! *(Sucks her teeth in disapproval.)*

VILLAGER 2: I want to know... Why us? If Seretse wants to do unfamiliar things, why does he not remain there in England? He is being a horror, I say.

VILLAGER 1: No! Why should he stay in England? He will do well to come here and consult us. We will advise him well. We are his people after all.

VILLAGER 4: I say, he has been in England for too long. I shit upon such radicalism.

VILLAGER 2: You hit the bull on the very horn, *mma*. What have you been quiet for? *Akanya hela* a white woman for our king's wife? Ah, we have not heard of such a happening.

VILLAGER 3: I say, is Kgosi Seretse trying to tell us that we are going to have princes and princesses of mixed blood? *Heeeei! (Claps her hands theatrically.)*

VILLAGER 1: Just imagine! I say, his Uncle Tshekedi must set him straight. That is if Seretse is indeed coming to Serowe.

VILLAGER 2: Don't let yourselves worry, my brothers and sisters. We will advise him on this very soil. *(She is standing with hands on hips, pointing sharply to the ground.)*

VILLAGER 4: From Sekgoma to Maphiri to Khama, this land has never even dreamed of such! And as our people say, the hind foot must always step where the front one did. So, we must advise Kgosi Seretse. I mean, does he want the South African Maburu to attack us for mixing black and white blood? Hmm... I say, Kgosi Seretse must not bring us trouble. He must not even try!

Scene 5
Kupasuka
("Rupture" in Kiswahili)

Transition. Back in the classroom. The class is in the middle of an exciting discussion about Sir Seretse Khama's interracial marriage.

TEACHER: You are right, children. Some people wanted the marriage. Many more did not want the marriage. And some were confused. Now, children, you must listen to this carefully. In order to solve this matter and end Bechuanaland's confusion —

Why am I saying Bechuanaland instead of Botswana, children?

AJANI: We were a British Protectorate back then and the British could not say Botswana.

TEACHER: *(Speaking slowly to make sure that the students understand.)* Good job, Ajani. As I was saying, in order to solve this matter and end Bechuanaland's confusion, Seretse and his guardian Uncle Tshekedi communicated by telegram. In the end they both decided that Seretse should come and speak to the tribe. Do you follow, children?

ALL STUDENTS: Yes, Teacher.

TEACHER: You, Tuelo! Why don't you play Uncle Tshekedi and tell us what happened in 1947? And since you are so good at imitating Sir Seretse Khama, Lefika, you can play Sir Seretse. We will need a volunteer to play Ruth's father and another to play Daniel Malan.

(Two students raise their hands to play Mr. Williams and Dr. Malan.)

("Bagammangwato ba ga Mabiletsa" is played on guitar without vocals. Lefika, now morphing into Seretse, puts on the trousers and jacket for the part. Tuelo does the same for his character. The STOP's in the text are used to denote the telegraphic style of writing and may be said or omitted. The rest of the ensemble joins in for the kgota scene where Seretse addresses the entire ethnic group.)

UNCLE TSHEKEDI: My dear Sonny, sending this telegram hoping you arrived safely in London (STOP) Everything well in Serowe (STOP) Your uncle and father, Tshekedi Khama

SERETSE: Dear Uncle, settling well in England (STOP) Feeling lonely sometimes (STOP) Not enjoying courses in Latin and Greek (STOP) Changing degree to law (STOP) Your nephew and son, Seretse

UNCLE TSHEKEDI: My dear Sonny, congratulations on settling well (STOP) May my brother's spirit protect you, his beloved son (STOP) Put work into studies and be successful at the end of the year (STOP) Law is good choice for our future leader (STOP) Your uncle and father, Tshekedi Khama

(Change of emotional beat. Perhaps a pause.)

SERETSE: Dear Uncle, I send greetings (STOP) Thank you for sending my allowance early (STOP) Happy to write with good news (STOP) *(Pause)* Her name is Ruth Williams (STOP) Your nephew and son, Seretse

UNCLE TSHEKEDI: Dear Sonny, suspending your allowance (STOP) You are Prince of Bangwato (STOP) You are going to be King (STOP) Your people cannot accept this (STOP) Formal signing of documents in England does not constitute your marriage as far as we are concerned no marriage exists (STOP) We accept nothing short of dissolution of that marriage (STOP) Our decision firm (STOP) Welfare of tribe paramount in this case (STOP) Repeat, formal signing of documents in England does not constitute your marriage (STOP) Your father, Tshekedi Khama

SERETSE: Dear Uncle, tribe and you important to me (STOP) Already married (STOP) Dissolution unacceptable (STOP) Ready to return with wife (STOP) Suspension of allowances being felt (STOP) I pay four guineas weekly (STOP) *Ke le ngwana wa gago*, Seretse

UNCLE TSHEKEDI: Dear sonny, allowances sent (STOP) Airfare to Botswana (STOP) For one passenger (STOP) Get ready to leave at moment's notice (STOP) I can only discuss your proposal personally after your arrival here

(Transitional music. Seretse bids Ruth farewell, who is teary-eyed. He is carrying a bag. Ruth occasionally fixes his clothing, e.g., tie and hat before she exits while Seretse is still speaking. She is overcome with emotion. Mr. Williams and Dr. Malan interrupt Seretse's thoughts as he speaks. Williams and Malan are flashbacks, sometimes in Seretse's mind and sometimes in Ruth's.)

SERETSE: *(Tenderly.)* Even as I journey away from you, you dare to see our future in my journey. Like the Biblical Ruth who never left. I love you, Ruth.

RUTH: I know you will return, my Seretse. Love is patient.

SERETSE: I hope I have the strength to face my tribe. I will be back to you, my wife.

MR. WILLIAMS: *(He speaks emphatically, in a Londoner accent. Loud interruption.)* We cannot allow this to go on! This affair is too much. I keep telling that to my daughter Ruth. It is a laborious affair and it has brought no one happiness. My daughter is not happy in it. Neither are you, Seretse. Not because you do not love each other... no. But because the odds are impossibly stacked against you two. They really are.

SERETSE: *(To Ruth.)* Ruth, even as I journey into this deep uncertainty —

RUTH: ...the embers of our love will burn.

(Longish pause.)

SERETSE: I will send you telegrams. The embers of our love will, yes, burn.

RUTH: We should be in touch. We must not float past each other like oil and water. Do not doubt yourself.

MALAN: *(Rude and loud interruption.)* I am Daniel Malan, Prime Minister of the Union of South Africa. We are not the only ones who find this interracial arrangement you two propose both disturbing and disgusting. So do a lot of the British people. Perhaps more significant is that the Africans themselves find this marriage unsettling and inconvenient for society. I hereby read a letter submitted to Prime Minister Winston Churchill's office from a South African.

(Reading.) To Winston Churchill. May the good God bless Dr. Malan — all his Cabinet. He, like Hitler, is trying to cleanse God's beautiful world while the filthy British public are do-

ing everything they can to foul God's beauty by supporting Ruth and Seretse. Mr. Churchill, should you listen to the misled British public, the devil will rule. Britain will be brought down in one hour. Signed, Miss A. Gleason.

Mr. Khama and Miss Williams, it is not just us as governments who see an error in this "union" of yours. Even simple civilians see the error.

SERETSE: *(To Ruth.)* I love you.

(They kiss. Ruth exits)

Wait for me in front of the embers of our love then, my Ruth, and when you cannot stand my absence any longer, throw these embers into the sky so that they may remain there and turn into stars to give me the light that will guide me back to you. For stars, like dreams, are visible from anywhere.

Scene 6
Osobola Otya?
("How Will You Manage?" in Luganda)

Seretse arrives in Serowe. It is November 13, 1948. Village gathering place, kgota. Musician starts playing a traditional instrument—perhaps a drum—announcing the beginning of the meeting and the arrival of Kgosi Seretse. Lights come up. Lefika, as Seretse, is standing upstage center facing upstage with back to the audience before he begins to speak, and turns around. The villagers who are upstage are facing downstage and the ones downstage are facing upstage to suggest a circular space. Ensemble should respond with hums, interjections, etc. Poet announces arrival of the King with a poem. Theatrical, ceremonial music during the poem. Extras may join the scene. Only some people yell Seretse's name in praise while others are unimpressed, even telling the rest to compose themselves and stop cheering.

POET: *Pula e kile ya na lephothophotho ko ga Mma Ngwato ngwaga wa 1921. Ya tatsa matsha le makadiba, megobe ya penologa, dinoka bo-Motoutse tsa tala. Ya toga ya phatalala ga sala seretse.*

Who is this descending from the flying bird from England,
land of angels?

VILLAGER 5: *(To another villager.)* This is not a celebration. It is a
confrontation. Why is this poet using glorifying language, *ne
betsho*?

ALL VILLAGERS: *(As if to shut Villager 5 up.)* Seretse Khama!

POET: *Ba ga Mmangwato ba re o dule ha o le Phuti o le boikobo jaanong
o hetotse mmala, o ta o le phomphokgwe yo o maithukutho mabe.*

Who is this, robed as King, striding forward in the defense of
his father's name?

ALL VILLAGERS: Seretse Khama!

POET: But, why is his face heavy, like that of one at a trial of his
honor? Why are his eyes red? Today we welcome back our
son and King, to hear what words he has for our ears. For I
am but a poet for the house of the King, I must sit and listen.
May the people rejoice!

ALL VILLAGERS: Seretse Khama!

SERETSE: *Ka go tulwe yo o emang a ipolele leina pele ke ta a simolola
ka gore, gongwe le a nkitse gongwe ga le nkitse, mme nna ke Seretse
ngwana wa ga Sekgoma yo okileng a bo a le Kgosi ya lona Bangwato.*

I am your Prince. *Ke ntse ke le ko moseja go ithuta. Ke bonye thuto
e e nnyennyane koo mme e kgolo le ta e nthuta hano, tsatsing jeno.
Bagolo, maikaelelo ame ga se go golola tou le maroo.*

In a nutshell, I am going to continue to put on hold my duties
as chief of our Bangwato tribe while I lead the country toward
independence.

VILLAGER 2: *Boipuso?* I beg, rather get to the point. Do not beat the bush. Do not run around with our heads! Our Prince, you know exactly what this meeting is about and flags and independence have nothing to do with it!

SERETSE: My elders, please lend me your ears. It is perhaps clear that I will become the first president when the time comes. And as the future first President of Botswana I would like us to give thought to having a good flag. We will get to other matters of the marriage later in this meeting. For these few minutes I would like to tell you my ideas as far as the matter of the flag is concerned. Perhaps then you will understand my marriage better.

(Pause.)

The colors that—

UNCLE TSHEKEDI: You are bitter because we will not allow you to jeopardize the integrity of our people. *O re todisitse matho thata, morwa-Kgosi!* This matter has scratched us by the fore paw.

VILLAGER 4: By the very, very fore paw! *Ija.*

VILLAGER 5: We Kalangas never even knew about the woman, yet many of our people are still under this Kingdom.

SERETSE: *Ke ne ke sa le todise matho bagolo mme ha le eletsa ke ka le rerisa gape ka ngwetsi ya lona—*

TSHEKEDI: *(Laughs mockingly.)* We will not let you unravel the fabric of our society and you are bitter about it?

Utwang ngwana yo, batsadi.
O ntse a nna ko Moseja ke mo ota. Gompieno ke yo o boela gae go ta go mpolelela dithamakgorwana!

VILLAGER 4: *Ija! Dithamakgorwana!*

SERETSE: I am not bitter. But I am frustrated. Because I am compelled to live in England, to lead my people toward indepen-

dence from abroad. *Rrangwane*, I have not yet been able to
find out what I have done wrong.

(Increasing urgency.)

I have been told that my marriage is contrary to native custom, but I can prove that it is not!

(Pause. Seeking to reason with elders, he resorts to Setswana.)

Ka jalo ke ne ke kopa gore le mo amogele ka mabogo oo mabedi.

VILLAGER 2: *Ga go kake ga direga!* This is an abomination. What
are you suggesting? And suggesting it so bravely at that! We
are here to remedy this situation not to exacerbate it. As our
people say, when the skins of drums fall off they are anointed
with fat. We are here for that. Not arguments. *E le gore* why
would we argue when we know the truth?

VILLAGER 4: What exactly are you asking us to do? We are almost starving because of crop failure this year and you want
to bring us more trouble?

VILLAGER 2: You did not even consult about this so-called marriage! I, personally, am bitter about this.

VILLAGER 4: What child marries without the presence of family?
Sekgoma's son, what king marries without his people?
Bagaetsho, it is no wonder that the gods have not given us rain
for our crops.

UNCLE TSHEKEDI: Very foolish of you, Seretse. Foolish indeed.
A king must have a big cloud of witnesses at his wedding. We
feel shame and disgrace. We are becoming the laughing stock
of peasants who do not even own an insignificant goat.

SERETSE: *Ke a itse.* I know. All I ask is that you accept her as my
wife, as part of our royal family. I realize that I did not consult you about the engagement, yes. What does that mean, my
elders? *Rrangwane* Tshekedi, just how will my divorce guar-

antee that we will claim our independence from the British? What would the people, the Bangwato, have me do?

(Pause.)

It has been said that I am a coward and that I ought to say out-right that I do not want to be chief; that my heart is not with you or with this country. But I cannot say that; it is not in my thoughts and it is not so. I cannot say it just so that you will think that I am a man. You are angry with me because I will not leave my wife, a woman that you do not want. I cannot force you to accept her.

UNCLE TSHEKEDI: Who married this woman to you? *Ra re* who married you to her? *Rona kana moruthutha wa kgang re o beile hela gone hoo.*

VILLAGER 5: Yes, who tied the royal headscarf around her head?

SERETSE: I have admitted that I married her against your will and you have told me that you will not allow her to come here. You have the power to do that. If the power had been mine she would already be here. I love my country and my people and I have told you that even though there is this dis-agreement, I still want to be your chief. You say that because of her I cannot be your chief.

(Almost menacingly.)

Were I to part from her today, become chief, and then take her up again tomorrow, you would not then tell me that I must leave the tribe. Then I would be on the throne and could do as I pleased. But I have not cheated you. I have given you this chance to rule me. You all say you do not want the woman. I have told you, I tell you now. I cannot leave her, I cannot leave her. I cannot.

UNCLE TSHEKEDI: Morwa Kgosi, this is about our culture. We have a way that things are done and that way must be followed!

SERETSE: *Setso sa rona ke a se itse mme ha e le gore re ka tshwarelela mo go sone re sa lebe diemo tsa rona ga ke sa bone mosola.*

(Self-pityingly and yet, dismissively.)

Go siame. Le tsere tshwetso ya lona. You want to banish me. *(In response to his uncle Tshekedi.)*

VILLAGER 2: *Ga o a kobjwa ke ope ha! Wa re o kobilwe ke mang?*

SERETSE: *Ke moka le nkobileng.* You won't allow me to bring Ruth here, but I am not going to live here without her.

(Irritated.)

I will be leaving to go back to England and I will do what I need to do for my nation ... from England.

(Tshekedi asks him to stop. Crowd mumbles.)

(Seretse is increasingly getting emotional to point of tears.)

TSHEKEDI: You even have tears in your eyes? How England has made you as soft as porridge!

(Crowd laughs.)

SERETSE: Every morning I wake up and read the newspapers, read these abominations, these shameful reports that try to stir up scandal in my life, and to separate me from my wife: "Young Botswana Chief Marries British Girl Without His Tribe's Consent!" "Seretse Khama—Botswana's prodigal son question mark." Am I not a man? Do I not suffer?

The Rhodesians are standing strong against my marriage and even call it an "unfortunate" marriage. The South African white supremacists have banned me and my wife from South Africa and their prime minister Daniel Malan told me to my face that my marriage is "disgusting." He told me that South Africa cannot afford to have an interracial couple ruling just across their border.

(Bows head out of respect.)

Pele ga gago ha ke hitha, Rangwane Tshekedi o seka wa nkalola.

(Silence.)

We cannot fight among ourselves; our enemies are at work.

VILLAGER 4: *Rra, rona* we want peace with our neighbors. You know they all have white regimes. What will they do when they hear that we permitted this marriage? Are we going to tell them not to speak in anger since we entered this matter with only one foot?

VILLAGER 2: Where will we run to?

SERETSE: *(Responding.)* Let them do what they want. Let the South Africans impose sanctions on us. Let them use their military forces against us but we will never support their racism.

(Pause, then epiphany.)

Bagolo bame, lekgota le le hano, our future flag. On a blue background representing water, the life blood of our desert nation, a large black stripe represents Botswana's black majority; two smaller white stripes represent the white citizens and neighbors with whom the Batswana want to live in harmony.

(Seretse walks downstage and delivers the following line to the audience with his right hand raised.)

Now, who among you approve of my marriage?

(Looks around. Long silence. After an even longer pause, members of the ensemble stand with their right hands raised in support and stand behind the weeping King. He reacts, still facing audience, and smiles and laughs through his tears.)

UNCLE TSHEKEDI: *(Livid that Seretse has won the popular vote in support of the marriage, Tshekedi orders the crowd to leave.)*

Phatalalang! Disperse! Disperse!

(Lights fade.)

Scene 7
Umtwalo
("Burden" in isiXhosa)

Daniel Malan and Ian Smith, Prime Ministers of South Africa and Rhodesia, respectively. They both have strong Afrikaner accents. They are addressing the audience.

MALAN: South Africa, it is I, Daniel Francois Malan, your Prime Minister. We have heard what is happening across the border in Bechuanaland. We are most concerned and repulsed.

SMITH: We despise what the people of Bechuanaland are doing against nature. It must stop at this very minute. Rhodesia, I am your Prime Minister, Ian Smith, and I seriously warn you: do not even dream of interracial unnaturalness here. Not in our beloved Rhodesia.

MALAN: What the Prime Minister of Rhodesia said to his Rhodesians, I repeat to my South Africans. Any of you who think black should mix with white should know that within these borders it is impossible, unlawful, and un-Biblical. It will not be allowed here. What is going on in Bechuanaland is nothing short of unnatural and I hope for your sake that the law is respected.

SMITH: A Black will always be a Black and inferior to the White man. If this marriage across the border in Bechuanaland is not unnatural to you all, shall we also marry animals then? It is disgusting.

MALAN: With due consideration for the necessity of assuring every European, including those in this region of Africa as well as those in Europe, of a proper and humanely reasonable standard of living, such affairs will not be tolerated. Any of you citizens who think that Seretse Khama is right to marry a white woman should leave this land and go live in Bechuanaland where such things happen.

SMITH: As Dr. Malan, Prime Minister of South Africa, has often said, the natives must be separate, the Indians and the colored people each separate, too. You see, a wise man once said: "Anyone who sees and paints a sky green and fields blue ought to be sterilized."

Scene 8
验收
("Acceptance" in Chinese)

Back in the classroom. The children put away the costumes and props from the reenactment.

TEACHER: Well done, class. I feel as if I was there myself. Hmm. *Ke a roroma!*

JUNG-HWA: So, teacher, if Sir Seretse Khama is dead, how will we learn more about him?

FRANK: Or we could also learn about the other heroes from smaller ethnic groups. Like the Bakgalagadi.

TEACHER: Frank Churchill of England, are you sick in the head?

(Teacher takes a deep breath.)

Superb question, Jung-Hwa. We can use imagination as I always say. Everyone say Ee-mah-jee-nay-shun.

ALL STUDENTS: Ee-mah-jee-nay-shun.

TEACHER: Really excellent question, Jung-Hwa. It is clear that *some* students will pass grade seven.

(*Then, taking a jab at Frank.*) As for others... Hm. Anyhow, let me tell you children. History is imagination. Hmm... But, how else can we learn about the founding father?

(*Students have no answer.*)

How about asking our elders?

LEFIKA: I... I... I... never knew my pa-pa...parents, teacher.

TEACHER: (*Taken by surprise.*) Not even your father, at least?

LEFIKA: No, teacher.

TEACHER: (*The first time we see Teacher being compassionate.*) Hmm... As I always tell people, it is not good for a boy child to not have a father to show him how to be a man.

(*Shaking off emotion.*)

Let us go back to the question, class. Think of the folktale. What did Morwa-Ngwedi do?

AISHWARYA: He took his cart to his father's...

AJANI: *Kgota.*

TEACHER: Yes, and what did he do next?

TUELO: He asked old people to give direction, Teacher!

TEACHER: Superb! Well done, Tuelo. You are really improving. But don't stop trying just because you have been improving.

(*Waving the stick in his face.*)

If you do stop trying, I will beat you. Hmm... Children, can you imagine what Lady Ruth would tell us today if we asked her about Sir Seretse Khama? What would she, as our elder, tell us about how she was welcomed to Serowe? About how the women of the village came in their brightly colored tuk-wis and special blue leteisi dresses to greet their Queen. How the women brought with them baskets of mabele, sacks of mmidi and bundles of mptshwe. Oh let me tell you children, it must have been a splendid sight indeed. I even wish I was there. I tell you, I would have been the one to put the tukwi on Lady Ruth. *Hei,* I can just see myself there. But I must tell you children that on that day of acceptance did not come easily. Hmm. I suppose you don't get harmony when everybody sings the same note.

(Transition music.)

Scene 9
Præget af Tro
("Characterized by Faith" in Danish)

Women of Serowe village are once again gathered to discuss village issues. This time they are at the river discussing King Seretse's marriage to a white woman while filling their buckets with water. Two lines of singing.

Lyrics:
Re Batswana mo Botswana... Iya o Iya o Hei Mmama
Iya o!
Re Batswana mo Botswana... Iya o Iya o Hei Mmama
Iya o!

VILLAGER 3: Are we not good enough? *Ija!* Tell me, my sisters are we not beautiful? Hmmm... This is most vexing.

VILLAGER 4: What are you talking about? You always do this when you have something to say. You beat around the bush until we actually pull the words from your throat. Spit it out at once, *mma.* It is almost sunset and some of us have porridge to put on the fire.

VILLAGER 1: Yes, speak and stop making our ears itch with

anticipation. You and your comedy! You think we are so rich as to stand here for nothing.

VILLAGER 3: Good grief, don't burn the hair off of my head already! Anyway, it is about our king. Of all the beautiful women in this kingdom, maidens with skin as smooth as butter, Seretse does not even choose one to be his wife. Are we ugly? Are we not good enough? Ah!

VILLAGER 2: *Hei, mma*. I am glad that you brought up this matter. It does not touch me right. I mean, do we have to have corn-yellow hair on our heads just to be good enough? Must we be pale before he takes a look at us? Women in this kingdom must not let this matter be taken lightly, I say.

VILLAGER 3: What will we tell our children? That our king married outside the kingdom because why? Hmm...

(Pause.)

In any case, we must not be stress-free about such foolish destruction of our kingdom.

VILLAGER 1: Me, I even saw the woman.

VILLAGER 4: You did?

VILLAGER 1: *Ee!* I did!

VILLAGER 2: Did she shake your hand?

VILLAGER 1: What? I did not even have the courage to greet her. Me, I am scared of white people.

VILLAGER 3: *Hei,* white people and their intimidating airs. Did she intimidate you?

VILLAGER 1: No. In fact, she seemed pleasant.

VILLAGER 4: Pleasant for what? I say, pleasant for what? Do not start with your unfamiliar ideas! That woman has no place here as queen. She should go and be pleasant elsewhere.

VILLAGER 2: If she came as a commoner like all these people come to our kingdom, like that writer woman, we would welcome her.

VILLAGER 4: Bessie Head.

VILLAGER 2: Yes, look how well we have welcomed Bessie Head even with her wayward ways, her shiny hair and light skin. She now belongs to Serowe. But for an outsider to come and seek to be queen is simply to put sand in our porridge.

VILLAGER 3: Tell us, *mma* since you saw the wife of our king, what does she speak?

VILLAGER 1: What do you mean?

VILLAGER 3: *Ka re* does she speak Setswana or English?

VILLAGER 1: She speaks English, of course. What sort of question is that?

VILLAGER 3: What language did she speak with all of you people who went to the palace to welcome her?

VILLAGER 1: I said English, are you deaf?

VILLAGER 4: *Hei!* We are done for!

VILLAGER 1: Some say King Seretse has even started drinking alcohol. I hear he is drinking hard even.

VILLAGER 4: We heard! Drinking so hard as though there is a message in the bottle.

(They all laugh.)

VILLAGER 3: We are finished! I say, if this white woman wanted to devastate our future generations so badly she might as well have brought Britain's brutal army to come here and destroy our wombs.

VILLAGER 2: *(Hands on head.)* Of all tribes on this gaspingly parched land, why should we be the ones to have a queen who does not understand anything about our ways and not even our language? Did we eat our totem? Did we insult the ancestors? I say, why us? Ah! I don't even want to set eyes on this woman, me! Ah! The whole fabric of this kingdom has been unraveled as Prince Tshekedi predicted. The sun will not rise tomorrow.

Scene 10
闘争
("Struggle" in Japanese)

Daniel Malan and Ian Smith addressing their countries again, warning them against copying Bechuanaland's endorsement of interracial marriages.

MALAN: All of us are co-responsible for this wrong impression Bechuanaland has that it can mix white and black blood, and I do not exclude my own political party, nor do I exclude myself personally. We must stop them. All of us. We as the Union of South Africa must correct Bechuanaland. We are all responsible to maintain order. All of us—European, Indian, Colored, or Native.

SMITH: There is no place for the Black in the European community above the level of certain forms of labor. And accepting a marriage as unnatural as this one means that Bechuanaland is trying to put the native into European culture. That is unacceptable and Rhodesia, you shall not welcome these noxious ideas from across the border. You would destroy our beloved Rhodesia.

MALAN: I trust that none of you citizens are irrational. I believe that you are not terrorists but guardians of this land, South Africa.

SMITH: We look at Bechuanaland with pity and repugnance as that godforsaken country slips into the abyss.

ACT 2
Prologue

Transitional music. Serowe villagers are bearing gifts in baskets. They are doing a ceremonial dance as they approach Ruth. The villagers are all women in this scene. Ruth is visibly pregnant. Once the elders have put all the gifts down and had their salutations, they begin to talk to Ruth. Two lines of singing to open this scene.

Lyrics:
Se nkgatele mosadi, ke mosadi wa dikgomo.
O a rekwa o a ithekelwa, o rekwa ka dikgomo.

VILLAGER 1: *(Putting a shawl or scarf over her shoulders.)* Our Queen, we see you. Welcome to Serowe, village of the two hills.

VILLAGER 2: Our Queen, we see you. We apologize that so few of us came.

VILLAGER 4: *(Tying a headscarf around her head.)* Our Queen, our Mother. Love bears all things, believes all things, hopes all things, endures all things. 1 Corinthians 13:7. May you live long.

VILLAGER 3: Our Queen, *Mohumagadi wa ga* Kgosi Khama. We apologize that so few of us came. Welcome to Serowe.

(They sit beside her.)

VILLAGER 1: Tell us, Mother, when the king was in Serowe defending the marriage, what was going on in your household in England?

RUTH: My sisters, we found ourselves in a difficult situation.

(Transition to flashback. Williams household. Ruth's parents are in the living room. Mr. Williams is reading a newspaper. Mrs. Williams is knitting. Simultaneously on the other side of the stage, Ruth is staring at Seretse's jacket in her arms, sobbing quietly. At the end of the scene, she clutches it close to herself and sobs audibly.)

MR. WILLIAMS: Are Ruth and Muriel not back yet? It's getting quite late.

MRS. WILLIAMS: No.

MR. WILLIAMS: When did they leave the house?

MRS. WILLIAMS: I am not certain but it was definitely after lunch. I think Muriel said they were going to stop at the London Missionary Society to pick up something.

MR. WILLIAMS: At the LMS? Pick up something at this time? Dear—

MRS. WILLIAMS: Yes, dear. What cause is there to worry?

MR. WILLIAMS: None. If she is meeting Seretse there, I certainly hope they both know that they are putting their lives in danger.

(Pause.)

I suppose you have not heard about the torrents of letters people sent to Churchill this past week?

MRS. WILLIAMS: More protest letters, I suppose.

MR. WILLIAMS: *(Reading from his newspaper.)* May the good God bless Dr. Malan—all his Cabinet. He, like Hitler, is trying to-cleanse God's beautiful world. Good grief! And here it says—

MRS. WILLIAMS: That is quite enough, dear.

MR. WILLIAMS: *(Puts down the newspaper.)* This affair—love and commitment notwithstanding—is certainly bringing us too much attention. Pain, really. Even the Prime Minister knows about our family. Oh, dear.

MRS. WILLIAMS: What are you suggesting?

MR. WILLIAMS: If only Ruth would let this go and give us peace!

MRS. WILLIAMS: Are you still suggesting that she and Seretse separate?

MR. WILLIAMS: Yes. That would bring peace to all of us. It is not as if they themselves are enjoying being spied on and running around tearfully doing this, that, and the other just to be able to hold hands in public.

MRS. WILLIAMS: I am afraid I don't believe separation is the answer anymore. They have shown me a possibility. I would like to be part of it.

MR. WILLIAMS: Are you enjoying this?

MRS. WILLIAMS: Enjoying? Are you joking? I think soon the British government will feel the pressure. There is enough support from the British public for this marriage.

MR. WILLIAMS: Well, there are enough people against this relationship too.

MRS. WILLIAMS: My husband—

MR. WILLIAMS: That letter I read from was written by a South African. Even the Africans are opposing this mixed marriage. Who are we to say otherwise?

MRS. WILLIAMS: By my reckoning, that letter was written by a *white* South African, not just any African. There is a difference.

Scene I
Huru-Hara
("Chaos" in Malay)

Back in the classroom. The teacher points to the students as she speaks about them.

TEACHER: Times were not easy, children. In those times you could not have a class like this. Look, Jung-Hwa's parents are Korean, Aishwarya's are Indian, Frank's are English, Lefika's are Tswana. You would not be allowed to mix like this in those days in our neighbor South Africa. And Sir Seretse made sure our land did not adopt that system.

MILDRED: I like it like this, Teacher.

TEACHER: Yes, we all do in this class, right?

ALL STUDENTS: Yes, Teacher.

TUELO: Teacher, I keep wondering if Sir Seretse and Lady Ruth ever enjoyed London just—

TEACHER: You mean without all the worrying?

TUELO: Yes... Yes, Teacher.

TEACHER: Excellent thought, Tuelo. These days you are improving so much that you are even starting to look nice! Hmm. I am sure they found time to enjoy music. Did you know that on their first date they went to a concert? I tell you children, they were musical. I am sure Ruth and I would have liked the same music. I mean Miriam Makeba, Ink Spots, Louis Armstrong. Ah, I can almost see myself being her best friend.

Scene 2
Go Senka Mothohatso
("To Seek Humanization" in Setswana)

The mood between Ruth and Seretse is playful, joyous, and crackling. He is waiting for her at the gate of the Williams residence in London. Ruth comes out dressed up and meets Seretse, who is also dressed up and wears a hat.

RUTH: I am finally ready to go. Pardon me for the delay.

SERETSE: All right?

RUTH: All right. *(She smiles at him, and shows him a shortcut to the concert.)*

RUTH: This way. It is the shortcut.

SERETSE: Ok. It is a very hot night for London, isn't it?

RUTH: Quite. Blimey! I was hoping that the rain would cool things a bit. But no!

SERETSE: That is what we are always hoping for back home. We are always hoping for rain.

RUTH: Because it's too hot?

SERETSE: Yes. But also for agriculture. For harvests. The color of prosperity, in my mind, is blue. Water. Rain. Good harvest.

RUTH: I like that. I also associate blue with... something calm, not tempestuous.

SERETSE: Thank you for agreeing to come with me tonight.

RUTH: You smell of cigarette smoke.

SERETSE: I apologize. Do you mind?

RUTH: So, you smoke?

SERETSE: I do.

RUTH: That is alright.

(Pause.)

Thank you for inviting me.

SERETSE: Thank you.

RUTH: You said you had two tickets to see the Ink Spots and that's my favorite band. How could I resist? You know, it is funny how you were when we first met at Nutford House.

SERETSE: It was a public gathering. With all the African students there who expect me to act in a certain manner because they are from home.

RUTH: And so?

SERETSE: And so, you have just got to know me better in the past four months, that's all.

RUTH: Why did it take you four months to ask me on a date?

SERETSE: Exactly what I said. So that you got to know me better. Besides, I was nervous.

(He laughs. His smile is wide and lovely.)

RUTH: You are more interesting than you were then. Such a charmer! That was the first time I had a conversation with someone from Africa. Do you ever see any of the African students whom my sister hosted that day?

SERETSE: I see Calvin and a few others, yes. How is your sister?

RUTH: She is well. She enjoyed meeting you then and she knows we are going to the concert tonight.

SERETSE: Very well. Is she worried we might get attacked?

RUTH: I don't think anyone will attack us. But yes, she is worried that we may get nasty looks, especially for dancing together.

SERETSE: Well, spirits have no color. Or maybe just blue.

RUTH: True. Though we may appear black or white, we are all blue.

(They pass workers sweeping the street.)

SERETSE: You know, it is still bizarre for me to see white people sweeping the streets like that. Back home, you would never see a white person doing that kind of work.

RUTH: They probably sit on their chairs with their fat stomachs and command the Black Africans, don't they?

SERETSE: They do.

(Pause.)

RUTH: Seretse.

SERETSE: Yes.

RUTH: *(Closing her eyes and holding onto him to stay walking on the path.)* What color are my eyes?

SERETSE: What? And why are your eyes closed?

RUTH: I will not open them until you tell me what color they are. For now you have to lead me because I cannot see.

(She puts her hand on his shoulder.)

SERETSE: Okay.

RUTH: What color are my eyes? It has been four months since we first met. So, I am just asking to see if you got to know me better in that time.

SERETSE: *(Taking her by the arm to guide her better with her eyes closed.)* And knowing you better equates to knowing the color of your eyes, you reckon?

RUTH: Part of it. What color are my eyes? I insist, I must get an answer.

SERETSE: Blue and green.

RUTH: What?

SERETSE: One eye is blue and the other is green.

RUTH: *(Opening her eyes.)* Seretse Khama, my dear gentleman, I am amazed! That is almost correct. One eye is grey-green and the other is grey-blue.

SERETSE: And voila, we are at the club.

(They enter the club. "If I Didn't Care" by the Ink Spots is playing.)

Listen, I know today is our first date but... do you mind if I have a pint tonight?

RUTH: You drink?

SERETSE: I do. I started when I moved to England.

RUTH: You? I would have never thought in a million years. I mean I can sort of see smoking. Hmm... you get more interesting every day.

SERETSE: Well...

RUTH: You are an honest man, I see. I might have a drink myself.

SERETSE: You drink? Do your parents know?

RUTH: What they do not know does not hurt them, does it?

SERETSE: It certainly won't.

RUTH: But they do know that you are black.

SERETSE: Oh dear.

RUTH: That is not going down well.

SERETSE: I cannot imagine it would. Hostility from both of our families. What a sad game that both of our families are playing. Our tears as libation to unknown gods.

(Pause. He extends his hand to ask her for a dance.)

Miss Ruth Williams, shall we dance?

RUTH: Mr. Seretse Khama. Yes, of course.

(Ink Spots song "If I Didn't Care" plays as they dance and look into each other's eyes, smilingly.)

Scene 3
Ndobolo
("Marriage" in Ikalanga)

Back to the classroom setting. The students are asking their teacher questions about the details of Sir Seretse Khama's wedding.

AJANI: Teacher, was there a wedding ceremony for Lady Ruth and Sir Seretse?

TEACHER: Yes. But it was not a big ceremony.

MILDRED: Why? He is a king!

TEACHER: A lot of people did not want to be seen there, even though they supported the wedding. They feared for their own lives.

FRANK: Isn't his legacy in other things as well, not just marriage to a white woman?

(Pause.)

AJANI: Teacher, you say people did not want to attend? I cannot imagine!

TEACHER: Well, it was difficult for them to get a priest who was willing to marry them. This was in England. When they eventually married, she wore a black dress for the day.

JUNG-HWA: Isn't a wedding gown supposed to be white?

(Transition to wedding scene between Ruth and Seretse.)

SERETSE: *(Calling out to Ruth from the kitchen.)* Darling, your breakfast is getting cold. Today is a big day. We must start the day with a good breakfast.

(Ruth enters, dressed in a black dress.)

RUTH: A very good morning!

SERETSE: Dear, why are you wearing black?

RUTH: I am wearing black for our wedding day, Seretse. *(Kisses him.)*

SERETSE: And why is that? I don't understand.

RUTH: Look me in the eyes. I have something to say.

(He turns to look at her.)

When you and I met, that day was... a gift. A gift to us from somewhere. It was the happiest day of my life. But since then our relationship has been hindered.

Barred. Opposed. Insulted. All that struggle has brought us deep agony and sometimes we felt as though everything would go pear-shaped for good. That struggle cast a shadow over a love so pure and simple. And today I wear this black to symbolize that never again will a dark cloud be cast over this marriage. Understand this black dress as the ultimate renewal of my commitment.

SERETSE: *(He kisses her.)* I hope it will be easy to explain to our children one day when they see our wedding pictures.

(They laugh.)

For all you have done and sacrificed for us to be together, you are simply my hero. And I will always be there to offer the hero a shoulder when she needs it.

RUTH: I cannot wait to be your wife.

SERETSE: You are my strength and weakness. I love you.

RUTH: I love you and I like you.

(Pause.)

Shall we have breakfast?

SERETSE: Yes.

Scene 4

قصص غير مكتملة
("Incomplete Stories" in Arabic)

Back to the villagers and their queen. The villagers are gushing from hearing about the wedding day.

VILLAGER 4: I live for such romantic stories, my Queen. If only my pudgy husband would express how he feels about me once in a while! That emotionless man of mine. Aaah! Modimoosi.

VILLAGER 2: Tell us Queen, what food does the king like?

VILLAGER 1: Is he good with children? Tell us, our Queen, tell us.

VILLAGER 4: I mean, if Modimoosi would just say "I love you" once in a while, it would make such a difference. *Ka re* these young men should learn a thing or two from how the king does it!

(*Laughter from all.*)

Anyway, our Queen, please tell us what King Seretse likes to eat.

RUTH: My sisters, you know your king and how he fills his pockets with dried phane worms and snacks on them!

(*Ruth laughs and the women join in.*)

(*Then, thoughtfully.*) He is a gentle soul yet he takes on the most difficult of tasks.

VILLAGER 1: And he is probably excellent with children, isn't he? Tell us, our Mother.

RUTH: Oh let me tell you, I remember when our first-born, Jacqueline, was a baby. We were living in London.

(*On the other side of the stage, Lefika enters into a soft spotlight as older Sir Seretse with a baby in his arms. Ruth speaks slowly as she reminisces. Lights fade on Lefika when the baby story is finished.*)

They were inseparable. He never rested. Seretse would hold her in his arms for hours. And baby Jacqui would sleep so peacefully until morning.

VILLAGER 4: You see, if only my husband would help me with the children once in a while

VILLAGER 2: Oh, our Queen, that is just how we know our king to be. He is a protector. It is no wonder that Jacqueline looks like him. He stared at her for too long when she was a baby. Don't all parents dream of that?

RUTH: *(Enjoying what Villager 2 just said.)* Because he doted upon her when she was a baby, she looks like him.

(Softer.) I quite like that. I like that.

VILLAGER 4: Tell us, our Queen, did the king ever attend school in Botswana?

RUTH: No. The protectorate was not very developed in terms of schools in his time. He attended Lovedale and Fort Hare in South Africa. There were many royals in those schools. And how he hated the way they behaved all puffed up!

(Re-enactment of Seretse's school days. Lefika is Seretse. It is supper time at Lovedale School. It is October 1, 1940. Ayanda, one of the Xhosa students at the school, walks over to the table where the Xhosa students of royal blood are seated. Ayanda is not a royal himself. Scene opens in school cafeteria.)

AYANDA: Bongani, can we use your salt? Our table has none.

BONGANI: You think you can just stand there and address me by my first name? I am a Xhosa prince. *Suka lapha!*

AYANDA: I am sorry, I know that you guys are royalty.

BONGANI: Standing there upright as a tree, not even bowing? Fall back!

AYANDA: Fine, I apologize. I apologize, Chief. Can we use your salt?

BONGANI: You know what? If I were indeed your chief, you would know how to address me, and I would indeed know to give you salt when you need it. Return to your table! *Uyadelela!*

(He puts his hand around the salt shaker to assert his power over Ayanda. Ayanda feels guilty and obediently trots over to his table).

SIPHO: *(Looking at Ayanda as Ayanda walks away.)* Nonsense. Civilian.

(Enter Seretse. He has been watching this conflict.)

SERETSE: Do you two think being royalty means you can treat people like that?

SIPHO: *Hei wena,* this is South Africa. If you want your foolish democracy you should not have come for secondary school in South Africa.

SERETSE: Part of being royal is knowing how to treat people. If you do not know that you are an idiot, royal or not.

SIPHO: Chap, if you do not mind people talking to you like you are not a royal, that is your problem. Don't involve us.

BONGANI: Exactly.

BONGANI: Acting as if they don't know who we are! Nincompoops.

(End of flashback. Back to Ruth and the Villagers.)

RUTH: That is typical Seretse. His religion is to do good. The world is his church.

VILLAGER 1: He sounds like the ideal—

RUTH: No. He is not perfect. Far from it, in fact.

VILLAGER 3: But tell us, Mother, how did you and the king meet?

RUTH: Remember that dinner for students coming from British colonies? That is where we met. That evening Seretse and I had the chance to be alone and talk.

(Flashback to Seretse and Ruth's first meeting. All the students from the colonies are gathered at Nutford House where Ruth's sister, Muriel, is hosting a dinner for all.)

SERETSE: Excuse me.

RUTH: Hello.

SERETSE: I am Seretse Khama from Bechuanaland.

RUTH: Ruth. I remember you from earlier.

SERETSE: Yes, when we spoke about jazz. I was wondering if there's a dustbin...

RUTH: For your serviette? Certainly. Please follow me.

SERETSE: Thank you.

RUTH: *(As they approach the dustbin.)* Voila!

SERETSE: Thank you.

RUTH: You are welcome.

SERETSE: It has been a good evening.

RUTH: You are not shy to mingle like most of the African students here.

SERETSE: *(Laughs.)* Well, there are reasons for that, one reckons.

RUTH: Such as?

SERETSE: Most of the African students here are frightened of white people, in awe of them because that is how they have been taught to behave.

RUTH: By whom?

SERETSE: In the colonies. By the missionaries.

RUTH: But you are different.

SERETSE: Well, Bechuanaland is different. Besides, in my mind I
am a lawyer and not a king.

RUTH: Most interesting.

SERETSE: I saw you trying to make conversation with my fellow
Africans earlier.

RUTH: I did.

SERETSE: Yes and they either cowered or were too polite to actually
converse, weren't they?

RUTH: Yes.

SERETSE: That is how those relations are socialized in the colonies.

RUTH: I am glad that now I can actually talk to someone at this
dinner. Again, I am Ruth.

SERETSE: I remember.

(They shake hands. They are obviously attracted to each other.)

RUTH: Between you and me, I have to say it feels liberating to talk
to someone who seems not to notice race.

SERETSE: We all notice race. But it does not have to take prece-
dence over other things. I suppose we believe in the same
thing then, you and me. It was a pleasure to meet you tonight.

RUTH: The pleasure is mine. Shall we go back inside for dessert with the others?

CALVIN: Hey! What are you two talking about?

Scene 5
Igihugu Ni Iki?
("What is a Country?" in Kinyarwanda.)

Back in the classroom.

AJANI: Teacher, I heard that when Lady Ruth first came to Serowe, some of the Khamas were scared of her because they
had never had a white person in their family.

MILDRED: Yes, I read it in *Mmegi* also.

AISHWARYA: Scared?

FRANK: I mean, it makes sense.

MILDRED: *(Sarcastically.)* Oh wow, Frank.

TEACHER: It could very well be. Where did you hear that?

AJANI: My aunt in Nigeria says she read it online.

TEACHER: Aishwarya, take my cup from the book cupboard and
get me cold water from the staff room.

AISHWARYA: Yes, Teacher.

(Aishwarya exits to fetch the water.)

TUELO: Teacher, did Sir Seretse Khama speak Setswana well?

AJANI: Yes, Teacher. Did he speak Setswana well?

TEACHER: Of course he did. What kind of useless question is that?

AJANI: But rich people don't speak Setswana.

MILDRED: Rich people speak Setswana.

TEACHER: *(Waving her stick energetically at Ajani.)* Who says?
You children need to learn to be proud of your languages.
Sir Seretse certainly was proud of his language. Those rich
Batswana you see who don't speak Setswana and walk like
this and speak English through their noses are just ignorant.
Don't be like that.

FRANK: Why do we not learn Kalanga in schools? Or Sesarwa?
How did they choose one language in this whole country to
teach it to all of us?

(Aishwarya walks in with the water.)

AISHWARYA: Here, Teacher.

TEACHER: It had better not be too cold. Every time I send you
children for water you put too much ice in it. Hmmm... wait
until you get to my age and your teeth will hurt when you
drink water that is too cold.

(All students except for Frank laugh. The teacher takes a sip.)

FRANK: I mean, drinking cold water is what makes teeth weak in
the first place so —

TEACHER: *(Hitting him very hard with the stick.)* Hei Hei! Get out of
this classroom! Go outside and stand in the sun! Stupid boy.

(Aside.) Because he is dull he has to talk all the time. Bloody
fool.

JUNG-HWA: Teacher, I was thinking I wish I had seen Sir Seretse
Khama when he was president.

TEACHER: *(Takes a moment to compose herself.)* Well, children, that
is why we study history. It allows us to time travel and meet

our heroes, isn't it?

ALL STUDENTS: Yes, Teacher.

TEACHER: Yes.

LEFIKA: In the folktale, the boy asks a woman for directions. Then he asks a man.

TEACHER: You read your own teacher's mind, Lefika.

(She sips her water.)

Where have you been hiding this intelligence? *Ija. Kooteng* we should make it Sir Seretse Khama Day everyday for you.

Scene 6
We Herinneren
("We Remember" in Dutch)

Transitional music. Teacher and students have invited former President Sir Quett Ketumile Masire into their classroom.

MASIRE: Thank you for inviting me to be part of your Sir Seretse Khama Day celebrations. I had the honor of working with the late Sir Seretse for many years as his Vice President and before that, as a comrade in the Botswana Democratic Party.

TUELO: Good morning, Sir Ketumile Masire. I would like to ask if you and Sir Seretse Khama were friends.

MASIRE: Absolutely. And when I became president after the unfortunate event of his death in 1980, I continued to learn from the way he had led when he was president.

MILDRED: Good morning, Sir Ketumile Masire. I would like to ask what memories you have of Sir Seretse Khama. Also, did he really have a battery in his heart?

MASIRE: Sir Seretse had a pacemaker, yes. Anyhow, this is one of my funny memories of Sir Seretse: when we first went to Nkange in the Bokalaka part of our country to campaign for the first elections of this republic, people of Nkange tried to say they could not join our Botswana Democratic Party before they had heard what the opposing party's message was. He said to them, "Then you may never join any party because the opposition has split. They are fighting over girls. *Gatwe ba lwela banyana ba* Girls Choir!"

(Laughter.)

Of course these memories now exist in fragments. First, I remember one day at the airport...

(Transitional music into Masire's memories of Seretse. For every short scene below, ensemble members take on different characters and react to what Seretse is saying. There is guitar music playing between each of these short scenes while the bodies on stage re-configure themselves. For example, for the airport scene, the other ensemble members should create a plane with their bodies and for the state address they should use their bodies to show a radio studio, etc.)

SERETSE: Thank you all for meeting me, my wife Ruth Khama, and my comrade, Ketumile Masire, at the airport on our arrival. My Uncle Tshekedi is also here.

TSHEKEDI: Thank you all for the encouragement you continue to give my nephew, Seretse. He and I have had our differences in the past, but as our people say, an elder must gain knowledge from the wisdom of the young. My dear Sonny, your beloved Seretse Khama, will do us all proud in the next chapter of our history. He will rid us of the Protectorate status and lead us to marvelous prosperity.

SERETSE: I did not say to eulogize me, *Rrangwane.*

(They share a hearty laugh.)

Anyhow, I wanted to tell our journalists here and the nation at large about our proposed coat of arms as the Botswana Democratic Party.

(Ensemble members arrange their bodies as a "sculpture" of the coat of arms. Sir Seretse explains it pointing at them as one would in a Power-Point presentation.)

The head of the bull needs no explanation: cattle were the mainstay of Bechuanaland's economy, and the eventual Republic of Botswana will continue to rely on cattle to a very great extent.

To represent the natural fauna of the country, therefore, two zebras and two elephant tusks have been included in the proposed design for the coat of arms. The zebras have been chosen out of all the wild animals which are found in the country, partly because they are not the totem of any particular section of the population of Bechuanaland, and therefore no preference is accorded to any particular section or group of people. In addition, the zebra is black and white, which represents the biracial character of the society we are trying to build.

(Transitional music plays to show time passing. Seretse moves to a different part of the audience to address them.)

For our currency, the word "pula"' needs little explanation. Rain is the lifeblood of our desert nation and pula is a well-known expression. It expresses a hope and belief that we will win elections and good fortune will be our partner in the years ahead.

(Laughter.)

(Transition to a roundtable where the BDP executives are seated in a meeting. Masire is present.)

We have a letter of congratulations from the Swedish Democratic Party. The vice president of our party, Masire, will brief you on that later; he says he forgot the letter in a jacket that he is not wearing today. I am just impressed that he has more than one jacket!

(Laughter.)

It was suggested by many people that if we get voted as
Botswana's first government, our party colors—red, black,
and white—should be adopted as the national colors of the
country. But I decided—with the support of Masire and the
committee—that more neutral colors and a more neutral flag
should be adopted: blue, black and white.

*(Private conversation between Ruth and Seretse moments before they
walk out into the crowds for him to be sworn in as president. Seretse is
nervous.)*

SERETSE: Love?

RUTH: Yes.

SERETSE: The country has voted for me as the first president.

RUTH: And I am proud of you. And so happy. You worked ter-
ribly hard.

SERETSE: I worked hard.

(Pause.)

Ah, I am so nervous.

RUTH: Now, just enjoy the ceremonies and steer the new republic.

SERETSE: *(Nervously.)* How do I know I am the right person for this?

RUTH: *I* know.

(Pause.)

One works hard for big moments and when they come, it is
overwhelming. You are the right man for the job. Look me in

the eye, dear. Like me, the children are proud of you.

(Pause.)

Let the embers of our love burn for you.

(Seretse looks her in the eye.)

You are the right man for the job. It is time to dance a new dance.

(They share a laugh. Orchestral version of Botswana national anthem begins. It has no vocals in it.)

(Ensemble stands in a V-shape. The mouth of the V is downstage and Seretse walks through the V formation with glasses on, coming downstage with right hand raised as he recites the speech.)

(Seretse may walk slowly but speak at normal pace.)

SERETSE: *Nna Seretse Maphiri Khama ke ikana gore ka boammaaruri le thwaahalo, ke ta a dira ditiro tsame le ditshwanelo mo maemong a a kwa godimo ke le mototomedi wa puso ya Botswana. Ke ta a dirisa dinonoho tsame go direla le go thokomela batho ba Botswana ko nte ga poiho gongwe kgobelelelo, lerato kana kilo.*

So help me God! We were taught to despise ourselves and our ways of life. We were made to believe that we had no past to speak of, no history to boast of. Botswana, it should now be our intention to try and retrieve what we can of our past.

We should write our history books, to prove that we did have a past; and that this was a past just as worth writing and learning about as any other. We must excavate our history, dress it up in pride, intelligence, and foresight, so that it may indeed come alive in our consciousness today. We must connect the present to the past, so that the future may be secured. The past can disappear, and a nation without a past is a lost nation, and a people without a past is a people without a soul.

In that spirit, *bagaetsho*, please join me and Mohumagadi First Lady Ruth Khama, and our father and Uncle Tshekedi Khama in spirit in wishing the newly-born Republic of Botswana much rain and prosperous harvests this year. *Go tswa ko makgobok-gobong a Okavango* in the north of our country, *go heta jaana ka dipane tsa Makgadikgadi* in the north east, *go atamela gaetsho Serowe, go kgabaganya sekaka sa Kgalagadi, go tshwara ko teng-nyanateng ko Tsabong* in the south, Batswana *betsho nelwang ke PULA!* May it rain!

(The ensemble does a brief celebratory dance with music.)

(Interview.)

BBC ANNOUNCER: Congratulations, Your Excellency and First Lady. We at the BBC are certainly happy to see the formation of the Republic of Botswana. Now, at this juncture in history, Botswana is the only country in the world with a national emblem that symbolizes racial harmony. Are you still bitter about the trouble you went through as a couple in order to stay together?

SERETSE: *(Talking to the children, who are offstage.)* Ian, what is that noise?

(We hear Ian say "Nothing, Dad.")

Will you close the door to your room?

(We hear Ian say "Yes, Dad" from offstage. Sound of door closing.)

Children. Excuse me. *(Laughter.)*

To answer your question: There was a stage when I was rather resentful of my exile, but I put the blame on the British government rather than on the British people, because I know that they have always supported me, and deplored the action of their government. I see no reason why because of that treatment I should jeopardize the interests of my country. This is the history of our nation as well. One day it will be revived

and told a long time after we are gone and we have become
spirits.

RUTH: We always had incredible support from the British people. We always appreciated it and as my husband said, the
entire drama is in the past and we are not bitter or resentful.
In some ways, it was necessary for that to happen, so that history's course may change for the better. And we were lucky
that Botswana's independence also came without any war or
bloodshed.

BBC ANNOUNCER: Your Excellency, are you worried that new
opposition parties will be forming? Any anxieties?

SERETSE: What does anxiety solve? Does it make one taller? Or
more capable? *(Laughter.)*

I think it's healthy to have an effective opposition, because
it keeps the government on its toes. I would like to have it,
although I am not going to do anything at all to create it. We
will never have a one-party state by act of government. It
is the intention of my government to influence neighboring
states and others, to show that black and white people can
live together quite harmoniously and work for the interest of
their country.

Scene 7
Zerwata ze ze Nkuro
("Many Dreams" in Yeyi)

Back to the classroom.

TEACHER: Well done, children!

ALL STUDENTS: Thank you, Teacher.

TEACHER: You see how beautiful history is?

ALL STUDENTS: Yes, Teacher.

FRANK: So, Sir Seretse wanted us to live together.

TEACHER: *(Having something of a loud epiphany.)* Yes, Frank! For once you are saying something worthwhile; wonders indeed happen! Oh, I see it now. *Heeei!* You children are a Standard 7 class of different skin colors. This is the dream that Sir Seretse had in mind. And it has come true in you. Ah. I see it now. I never thought that we, sitting here, were the tapestry that Sir Seretse wove! Look! Straight hair, kinky hair, blonde hair, brown skin, black skin, white skin: Botswana is all of us. Hmm... Thank you, Frank.

FRANK: Maybe you also don't have to be so strict on us either. You are a good teacher so we understand without the cane.

JUNG-HWA: Yes, Teacher. No more stick.

TEACHER: Alright, children. Aishwarya, take my stick and throw it out of the window.

(Aishwarya breaks the stick and throws it out the window. Other students laugh and talk among themselves, happy.)

TEACHER: Yes, no more beating. But I have to say that you children are lucky I love Sir Seretse and Lady Ruth. Otherwise I would keep that stick. But if we are their dream tapestry, the stick must be replaced by other ways of teaching, just like the old should give way to the new, isn't it?

ALL STUDENTS: Yes, Teacher.

TEACHER: Most powerful. You children have taught me today. How imaginative you all are. Anyhow, you must tell all your bad-tempered friends on the playground what you learned today, okay? Now, take all the costumes and props and put them in the cupboard, everyone. Superb work.

(All the students take off the acting costumes and put the acting material in

the cupboard except for Lefika, who remains standing down stage facing audience with a crestfallen expression on his face. Everyone exits and when the teacher comes in with keys to close the classroom, she sees Lefika standing in silence. She stands behind him and speaks. He does not turn around.)

TEACHER: What is it, Lefika?

LEFIKA: I don't want to take off the costume, Teacher.

TEACHER: Did this remind you of your own father?

(Pause.)

LEFIKA: Can I keep this jacket, Teacher?

TEACHER: *(Realizing how much this means to him to find a father figure in Sir Seretse.)* Yes, Lefika. You may keep the entire costume.

(Softly.) Please lock the classroom and take the key to the staff room when you leave.

(Teacher leaves. Lights go out on the rest of the stage except on Lefika.)

LEFIKA: Seretse Khama, the sound of my drum. You were too young when you left. And so, to us, you will always be young, gifted, and handsome. I speak your name. Your spirit marches in my core, defiantly, and in your name I hear the proud sound of drums. I am the boy in the folktale. And the clouds are where your name was.

(Lights start to fade.)

King, in me, live again. Through me, dream again.
Botswana, in me, live again. Through me, dream again.
Botswana, in me, live!

THE END

MOTSWANA: AFRICA, DREAM AGAIN

PRODUCTION HISTORY

Motswana: Africa, Dream Again was first performed on November
17, 2012 at the United Solo Festival, the world's largest solo theatre festival, in New York City. It was presented as a solo play
written, directed, and performed by Donald Molosi.

Motswana premiered in Botswana in late 2013 as a two-hander
starring Donald Molosi in one of the roles. Since then, the play has
been performed across North America. In 2015, *Motswana* toured
Botswana and South Africa and returned to the United Solo Festival for an encore performance.

AWARDS

In March 2013, *Motswana* was selected for online publication by
Indie Theater Now, a prestigious online database of plays. The
play has been reviewed in *The New York Theater Review* and other
prestigious Broadway publications.

PLAYWRIGHT'S NOTE

For obvious reasons, nation states usually promote only a singular streamlined national identity of themselves, thus neglecting the story of said nation's heterogeneity. In *Motswana: Africa, Dream Again* though, I wanted to explore the somewhat homogenous national identity of Botswana through the stories of Botswana's own ethnic diversity. *Motswana* discusses not the cohesiveness of a nation but the points of slippage, where intranational diversity implodes and exposes the limitations of the umbrella concept of a nation, and whether one can truly come from a nation if a nation is an unfixed idea. Nations are constructs; they expand and contract, and sometimes disappear.

"Motswana" simply means "citizen of Botswana." The Republic of Botswana is often called Africa's golden example for its enduring democracy and relative wealth. This multilayered multilingual play satirically and docu-dramatically asks:

1) Who, exactly, can confidently claim to be a Motswana?

2) What unexpected revelations about the Motswana identity surface once we acknowledge that African borders were fabricated not in aid of the cohesion of African nations but to serve colonialism?

3) Given the migratory nature of African peoples before the invention of borders on the continent, is "Motswana" a misnomer for describing Botswana nationals?

Parts of the script are adapted from actual speeches by President Thabo Mbeki, Philly Lutaaya, and President Seretse Khama. Yvonne Vera's work on Chaminuka and Nehanda also inspired certain parts.

***

This play is dedicated to my dear mother, Gosego Nnananyana Molosi, who is my ultimate Motswana.

—Donald Molosi
Gaborone, Botswana
October, 2015

CAST OF CHARACTERS

PAPA/TIMOTHY ZIBANANI GULUBANI: Patriarch of the Gulubani family. He is in his sixties. He is a conservative politician who earned his wealth from a long political career.

MAMA/CECILIA GULUBANI: Matriarch of the Gulubani family. She is in her early fifties and is a devoted mother and wife. She does not enjoy her job at the office.

BOEMO GULUBANI: Thirty-year-old man with unconventional ideas. He is a Member of Parliament and lives with his parents.

UNCLE TSHEKEDI: Seretse Khama's uncle and guardian. He is in his forties and is both a disciplinarian and a devout Christian.

SERETSE KHAMA: Founding President of Botswana. In this play he's portrayed at age 27. He is passionate, diplomatic, and visionary.

CHAMINUKA: The ancestral spirit who visits to avenge his fellow Africans against colonizers. His age is timeless.

NEHANDA: The ancestral spirit who visits to avenge her fellow Africans. This is the spirit-wife of Chaminuka. Her age is timeless.

PHILLIP "PHILLY" LUTAAYA: He is the first African to declare he has AIDS. He is portrayed in this play at age 38.

NOTES ON SET DESIGN AND COSTUMES

The non-English lines must be performed as written in the script alongside the English. Simple costume changes are recommended in transition between characters. Live music on the guitar and/ or drums is also recommended. Although this play was initially presented as a solo play, it may be performed with more actors as an ensemble piece.

MOTSWANA: AFRICA, DREAM AGAIN

by
Donald Molosi

How can I come from a nation?
How can a human being come from a concept?
—Taiye Selasi

Scene 1: These Young Generations

Upbeat Botswana music begins to play. As lights come up, Mama is already on stage setting the table. Papa enters. He is older and he walks with a limp. Papa and Mama are about to have supper.

PAPA: Cecilia my wife, I have been telling you, eh? This son of ours is what? Too much. Hmm...

(Pause.)

What is with this daft generation and their questions, anyway? Did questions ever fill any man's stomach? Do questions not just pour water onto simmering fat? I say, gone are the days when children were manageable, and believed what you told them they were, full-stop!

(Pause.)

Boemo is too much.

(Mockingly imitating Boemo.) Heei, I am half Kalanga and half Ngwato! *Hei wee,* I am one quarter Shona and one eighth Xhosa! *Hei wee* this! *Hei wee* that! Nincompoop.

(Romantically reminiscing on the past.)

In my day you were told that you took your father's identity and that was that. None of this *matakala* and noise and debate.

(Actor sucks his teeth as Papa and then transforms into Mama. She is calm and at first sight she seems to be feminine in a quiet, traditional way.)

MAMA: Must you really be this outraged by it? Certainly you cannot deny that our son is all those things. At least we in this country are fortunate enough to know our ancestral history, unlike our brothers and sisters across the ocean.

PAPA: Eh-eh. Tell me *mmaabo,* what man would have a totem if we all chose to be so many things at once? Would the tribes not disappear? I beg. This is not a light matter, my wife.

(He takes a sip of his scotch.)

MAMA: *Ah, rraabo.* Let the boy be. *Ga ke re* to call oneself a Motswana is not to call oneself not-Zimbabwean, not-Namibian, not—

PAPA: Ah-ha! You agree with him?

(Calling out.) Gods! Even my own wife is testing me today? Kalanga Gods of Gulubani, do you hear my lamentations? *Heei!*

(Clapping hands theatrically.)

My wife, if I am hearing you correctly... you are confessing that Boemo's ideas are entering your head.

MAMA: *(Slightly amused by his melodrama.)* Do lower your voice, my husband. Boemo might hear you from his room.

(Reasoning with him.) Listen, you must cool your head before anything can be solved. As our fathers say, no matter how hot your anger is, it cannot cook a potato.

(Crosses to him.)

Now listen, father of my children. I am only trying to tell you what you already know, which is the fact that our ancestors moved freely across all these savannas. All these lakes. All these hills. Why then would what Boemo says be strange?

PAPA: Eh-eh! I refuse. What does that make me? Or you?

MAMA: Who knows? I am just saying that the new generation might not be altogether nonsensical.

PAPA: This is too much. I mean, does Boemo think he is the boss of us? Does he actually think that he—

Hmm...

Colossians 3:20 says, "Children, obey your parents in everything, for this PLEASES THE LORD!" Yet my son's questions
continue to rub mud in my face.

MAMA: The same bible that demonizes your Gods of Gulubani, eh?

PAPA: *(Long pause. Papa sighs.)* Let us eat our supper in peace, my
wife.

(Lights fade.)

Scene 2: Ode to Thabo Mbeki

*Atmospheric percussion plays. Boemo rises from the ground as though
sprouting from the earth like a seed. He speaks with feeling and with a
slow urgency. Throughout the play, Boemo speaks out loud while scrib-
bling in his journal.*

BOEMO: I am an African. At the same time I am a Motswana. I
owe my being to the hills and the valleys, the mountains and
the glades, the rivers, the deserts, the trees, the flowers, the
seas, and the ever-changing seasons that define the face of our
native land.

My body has frozen in our frosts and in our snows. It has
thawed in the warmth of our sunshine and melted in the heat
of the midday sun. The crack and the rumble of the summer
thunders, lashed by startling lightning, have been a cause of
both trembling and hope. Nature's fragrances have been as
pleasant to us as the sight of blooming flowers.

The dramatic shapes of the Drakensberg, the soil-colored
waters of the Okavango, the perennial Zambezi, and the timeless sands of the Kgalagadi are all panels on the natural stage

where we act out the theatre of our day.

At times, and in fear, I have wondered whether I should concede equal citizenship of our countries to the leopard and the lion, the elephant and the springbok, the hyena, the black mamba, and the pestilential mosquito, for there exists a human presence among all these. A feature on the face of our native land thus defined. I know that none dare challenge me when I say, I am an African.

I owe my being to the Khoi and the San, Basarwa of the seventeenth century whose desolate souls stalk the great expanses of the beautiful Cape, haunt the epic Chinoyi Caves, and march the majestic Makgadikgadi. They who fell victim to the most merciless genocide our native land has ever seen. They who were the first to lose their lives in the struggle to defend our freedom and independence. Like the Hottentot Venus.

PAPA: Son, do you mean Saartjie Baartman?

BOEMO: Yes.

(Regaining his thought.)

They who were first to lose their lives in the struggle to defend our freedom and independence. Like Saartjie Baartman, whom the French exhibited in a cage like a wild animal. Ota Benga, whom the Americans exhibited in a New York City zoo as a specimen of an African pygmy until he could no longer bear the humiliation and took his own life. El Negro de Banyoles, the Mothaping King whose body the French exhumed, eviscerated, and stuffed in the same way as a trophy animal and then gave to a Spanish museum to exhibit.

Today, as a people, we are audibly silent about these ancestors, fearful to admit the horror of a former deed, seeking to obliterate from our memories a cruel occurrence, burying our histories with the bones of our ancestors.

(Pause.)

I am formed of the Tswana people who ruled the land between the Okavango and the Vaal rivers. I am formed of the Kalangas ba-ka Nswazwi, of Mujaji the Rain Queen. I am formed of migrants who left Europe to find a new home on our native land. Whatever their actions, they remain part of me.

In my veins courses the blood of the Malay slaves who came from the East. Their proud dignity informs my bearing, their culture a part of my essence. The stripes they bore on their bodies from the lash of the slave master are a reminder embossed on my consciousness of what should not be done.

I am the grandchild of the warrior men and women led by Kgosi Khama and Kgosi Sechele, the patriots that Mbuya Nehanda and Sekuru Kaguvi took to battle, the soldiers that Kgosi Moshoeshoe and King Shaka Zulu —

PAPA: Son, do you mean Nkosi Shaka Zulu?

BOEMO: Yes. The soldiers that Kgosi Moshoeshoe and Nkosi Shaka Zulu taught never to dishonor the cause of freedom.

(Beat.)

My mind and my knowledge of myself are formed by the victories that are the jewels in our African crowns, the victories we earned from Lagos to Juba, from Dimawe to Sophiatown, as the Ashanti of Ghana, as the Berbers of the Sahara, as the Swahili of Tanganyika. Being part of all these people, and in the knowledge that none dare contest that assertion, I shall claim that I am an African. And I am a Motswana.

Scene 3: State of the Nation

Papa and Mama. This time they are not eating but doing different actions around the house. She is absent-mindedly reading a newspaper while watching television and occasionally flicking through channels. Papa is opening mail with a letter opener and occasionally pauses to skim the letters.

MAMA: *Ijaa!* The news these days! Why is it on the front page that a cabinet minister slept with two young women at the same time?

(Looking up from the newspaper and pausing to look at the TV.) Is this news? They are showing that plump beauty queen again? Someone tell me what I am looking at.

PAPA: I tell you these days all things are tumbling into rough weather.

(Laughing.) Look at her chew her tongue, this professed beauty queen. The girl threatens to fall asleep mid-sentence. *(Laughing some more.)*

MAMA: Is this beauty?

PAPA: She is a dunderhead! Nincompoops. All of them. I shit upon such radicalism.

MAMA: *(Looking at her newspaper.)* Really, how about they put Motsamai Mpho on the front page? He founded this republic and even named it. And now he just died and there is barely any mention of—

PAPA: My wife, gone are the days of good journalism. The days of Rampholo Molefhe. Russ Molosiwa. Those were the days. Sometimes I think that after the British left we plunged into mediocrity.

MAMA: *(Showing Papa a newspaper article.)* And look at this, they mistakenly published Kenneth Kaunda's eulogy while he is still alive!

PAPA: Nincompoops.

MAMA: *(Smacking the newspaper.)* And this woman is dancing around in her panties telling people that she has sexual desires for President Ian Khama. I am finished with this newspaper!

PAPA: People these days love to read about decay. Ignoramuses. These media are the reason our son Boemo maintains this foolish talk of having ancestors across our borders. This kind of chatter enrages me. Gods, did I not send him to English Medium schools? Yet, he disgraces me.

MAMA: Come off it, *rraabo*. Perhaps no one will even read his bloody memoir.

PAPA: This boy will lose his seat in Parliament. I repeat, *mmaabo*, a fly that does not listen follows the dead body into the grave.

MAMA: Ah-ah, no more! We are not talking about that boy again, my husband.

(Mama opens the display unit to take out special wine glasses. She takes out a bottle of wine from the fridge.)

At least this whole business makes him curious about history.

(Smiling.) Anyway, my handsome husband, let us enjoy this Sunday afternoon with a nice splash of chardonnay.

PAPA: *(Pulls a gift from under the sofa and gives it to her. Pause.)* Happy anniversary, my wife.

MAMA: *(Gleeful.)* You remembered? Happy anniversary, Zibanani, father of my children.

(They kiss.)

PAPA: Genesis 2:24. "Therefore a man shall leave his father and his mother and hold fast to his wife, and they shall become one flesh." You are still all I could dream of, my beautiful mermaid.

MAMA: Twenty-six years.

PAPA: Yes. And still going so strong.

MAMA: *(She sings a verse from a Shania Twain song she likes, "You're*

Still The One." She sings pretty well. She gets a little theatrical with her gestures and moves with the song, but her sincerity is true. After a couple of lines of singing a cappella, the live musician joins in with guitar.)

Ain't nothin' better. We beat the odds together. I'm glad we didn't listen. Look at what we would be missin'. They said, "I bet they'll never make it." But just look at us holdin' on. We're still together, still goin' strong. You're still the one I run to. The one that I belong to. You're still the one I want for life.

(She has a little giggle fit and takes a mock bow. He claps.)

Zibanani, do you remember our poem from our first anniversary in Serowe?

PAPA: Of course.

MAMA: *(Teasing him.) Kana,* you used to be romantic.

(Shooing him teasingly when he tries to embrace her.)

Ah, leave me. *Ija,* do you even remember that sweet-sweet poem?

PAPA: *(Pause, and then he begins to recite. Perhaps, a little strumming on the guitar in the background.)*

Chobe, Gcwihaba, and the Linyanti—all of them ethereal, *moratiwa.* Beauteous and timeless.

MAMA: From the Tswapong Hills to the sands of Struizendam— all of them ethereal, *moratiwa*: beauteous and timeless.

PAPA: Still my favorite place in Botswana is in this marriage with you. *Ndokuda.*

MAMA: *Ke a go rata.*

PAPA: Prayerfully do we recite this, therefore that we may grow old together like a folktale and its lesson.

MAMA: That we may hold steadfastly onto this marriage the way that Bangwato proudly hold onto Serowe.

(They kiss.)

Scene 4: Motswana

Upbeat Botswana music begins to play as the actor changes into Boemo.

BOEMO: Place of birth? The town of Mahalapye, central Botswana. Full name? Boemo Timothy Gulubani. Height? One meter, 64 centimeters. Nationality? Motswana. That is what my passport says.

Motswana. It is a word used to refer to someone one belonging to one of the Tswana ethnic groups like Bakwena, Bangwaketse, Bangwato, and others—they are all Tswana people with totems ranging from crocodile to duiker to buffalo. But since these Tswana groups form the majority in the Republic of Botswana, every citizen in the country has to refer to themselves nationally as a "Motswana." How can we be stress-free about this issue? I have to call myself by that word, Motswana, a word that defines the country only by its ethnic majority. That is the very sand in my porridge; I have to call myself by this word that denies my father's ethnicity. We must not season this bitter issue with sweet lies and so I shall speak.

My father's side is Kalanga, definitely not a Tswana group. Totems there range from birds to animal hearts to whetstone. As I wrote in the previous chapter, my mother's side is Ngwato and therefore Tswana. But—according to some— since a child always takes the ethnicity of the father, I am not then ethnically a Motswana. This is no small madness!

Motswana is part of myself and, like stagnant water, I cannot run from myself. But instead of keeping a bruised silence, I often wonder out loud what would happen to that word, Motswana, if we imagined the southern African region without borders. Would the land not bloom with mobile citizens and fecund consciousnesses?

I always conclude that I could own that term—Motswana—only if I choose to see it as a diaspora, a more elastic and more inclusive identity: as a people that lie in the still-colonial territory I was born in as well as on the outskirts, in the so-called "neighboring countries" and so-called "other countries." That definition of Motswana does not cough out my Kalanga ancestry, you see. That understanding of the word ensures that everyone within these borders can have a hero. That is the Motswana that no one can Other.

Let me start with my mother's side, the Tswana side. She comes from the Bangwato ethnic group, the largest ethnic group in Botswana, one of the several in the country that can rightfully call themselves ethnically Motswana. Interestingly, Bangwato were the first Botswana ethnic group to approve of an interracial marriage when, in 1948, their King Seretse Khama married a white English woman, Ruth Williams, in London. King Seretse's guardian, Prince Tshekedi Khama, was opposed to the marriage and asked Seretse to return home from England to justify his unusual proposal before the entire ethnic group. And when, on November 13, 1948, the Bangwato accepted this interracial marriage and welcomed the prospect of mixed-blood royals, the definition of Motswana, as far as I am concerned, was immediately made elastic in a new way. It was expanded beyond race.

(Traditional Botswana guitar music begins to play.)

Scene 5: Seretse Khama

The following scene begins with a correspondence by telegram between Seretse Khama and his Uncle Tshekedi. "STOP" denotes the punctuation in a telegram. It can be said out loud in performance or omitted as the director chooses.

TSHEKEDI: My dear Sonny, sending you this telegram hoping you arrived safely in London (STOP) Everything well in Serowe (STOP) Your uncle and father, Tshekedi Khama

SERETSE: Dear Uncle, settling well in England. Feeling lonely sometimes. Not enjoying courses in Latin and Greek (STOP) Changing degree to Law. Your nephew and son, Seretse

TSHEKEDI: My dear Sonny, congratulations on settling well (STOP) May my brother's spirit protect you his beloved son (STOP) Put work into studies and be successful at the end of the year (STOP) Law is good choice for future leader (STOP) Your uncle and father, Tshekedi Khama

(Long pause.)

SERETSE: Dear Uncle, I send greetings (STOP) Thank you for sending my allowances early (STOP) Happy to write with good news —

(Pause.)

Her name is Ruth Williams (STOP) Your nephew and son, Seretse Khama

TSHEKEDI: Dear Sonny, suspending your allowances (STOP) You are Prince of Bangwato (STOP) You are going to be chief (STOP) Your people cannot accept this (STOP) Formal signing of documents in England does not constitute your marriage, as far as we are concerned no marriage exists (STOP) We accept nothing short of dissolution of that marriage (STOP) Our decision firm (STOP) Welfare of tribe paramount in this case (STOP) Repeat: Formal signing of documents in England does not constitute your marriage (STOP) Your father, Tshekedi Khama

SERETSE: Dear Uncle, tribe and you important to me (STOP) But already married (STOP) Dissolution unacceptable (STOP) ready to return with wife (STOP) Suspension of allowances being felt (STOP) I pay four guineas weekly for my flat

(STOP) *Ke le ngwana wa gago,* Seretse

TSHEKEDI: Dear Sonny, allowances sent (STOP) Airfare to Botswana (STOP) For one passenger (STOP) Get ready to leave at moment's notice (STOP) I can only discuss your proposal personally after your arrival here

("Bagammangwato Ba Ga Mabiletsa" or another song of the director's choice begins to play on guitar as actor puts on jacket to perform Seretse's justification of his marriage in Serowe, 1948.)

SERETSE: *Ke ne ke sa le todise matho bagolo mme ha le eletsa keka le rerisa gape ka ngwetsi ya lona—*am not bitter. But I am frustrated. Because I have been banned and I am compelled to live in England, to lead my people toward independence from abroad. *Rrangwane,* I have not yet been able to find out what I have done wrong.

(Increasing urgency.)

I have been told that my marriage is contrary to native custom, but I can prove that it is not!

(Pause. Seeking to reason with elders, he resorts to Setswana.)

Ka jalo ke ne ke kopa gore le mo amogele ka mabogo oo mabedi.

(Pause. Elders oppose the idea of this marriage.)

Bagolo bame, ga ke dirise—

(Elders cut him off and, to his surprise, they are more opposed than before.)

Ke a itse. I know. All I ask is that you accept her as my wife, as part of our royal family. I realize that I did not consult you about the engagement, yes.

(Pause.)

What does that mean, my elders? *Rrangwane* Tshekedi, just how will my divorce guarantee that we will claim our independence from the British?

(Pause, and then asking genuinely.)

What would the people, the Bangwato, have me do? It has been said that I am a coward and that I ought to say outright that I do not want to be chief, that my heart is not with you or with this protectorate. But I cannot say that; it is not in my thoughts and it is not so. I cannot say it just so that you will think that I am a man. You are angry with me because I will not leave my wife, a woman that you do not want. I cannot force you to accept her. I have admitted that I took her against your will and you have told me that you will not allow her to come here. You have the power to do that. If the power had been mine she would already be here. I love my country and my people and I have told you that even though there is this disagreement, I still want to be your chief. You say that because of her I cannot be your chief.

(Menacing, desperately.)

Were I to part from her today, become chief, and then take her up again tomorrow, you would not then tell me that I must leave the tribe. Then I would be on the throne and could do as I pleased. But I have not cheated you. I have given you this chance to rule me. You all say you do not want the woman *youdonotwantthewoman!*

I have told you, I tell you now. I cannot leave her, I cannot leave her. I cannot—

Scene 6: Across the Color Line

BOEMO: After that one event, the Motswana identity ceased to be about color. But that did not squash inequality.

My father's Kalangas are a minority in Botswana and their language is not taught in schools or used in journalism: in many ways they get the opposite treatment of what my mother's people get.

Whereas my mother's ethnically Tswana people are dominant in politics, my father's Kalanga people are not. While ethnically Tswana figures appear with smirking faces on every denomination of our pula, no Kalangas or non-ethnically-Tswana figures are recognized in the same way, despite their contributions to the creation and sustenance of this republic.

So, within the borders of Botswana, I am from both the dominant group as well as the subaltern. And thanks to our chronically colonized curriculum, I know little about the subaltern side. But I do know some things about the Kalangas' cousins, the Shona, who are mainly found in modern-day Zimbabwe. It seems, therefore, that to be a Motswana is to have those gaps in knowledge of one's roots, those silences.

We are told that when the Europeans came with the Bible in 1881 they sought to erase all religions that existed among my father's people. We are also told that that is when the spirit of Chaminuka found a medium in a man by the name of Pasipamire. The spirits of our ancestors spoke through him and in the process protected beliefs of all the people in the land, whether Shona, Ndebele, Tswana, or whatever else.

Like two peas in a pod, the spirit of Chaminuka is always accompanied by that of Nehanda. The story of Nehanda is always a reminder that the moment an African turns against another, our downfall is certain. Our condition is that delicate. Xenophobia should seem almost suicidal. More in the next chapter.

Scene 7: Ode to Yvonne Vera

Atmospheric music ushers in Chaminuka. The live musician says the shared lines with the actor, if the play is presented as a solo.

CHAMINUKA: I am the spirit Chaminuka. My God lives up above. He is a pool of water in the sky. My God is a rain-giver. I approach my God through my ancestors and my *mudzimu*. I brew beer for my god to praise him, and I dance. Tell them that, child. What kind of god is theirs that he will not be appeased with beer poured onto the ground?

CHAMINUKA AND NEHANDA: Chosen child, do they even know that if they killed you a patch of grass as large as your head would appear on the ground where you would then fall forward and join us? Do they?

CHAMINUKA: Agitator of the magnificent downfall of the Barozwi and the Matebele! Spirit of the proud land between the rivers of Limpopo and Zambezi! I AM CHAMINUKA! Owner of the land, commander of the wind! I know everything and nothing is impossible to me!

Tell them, child, that I, Chaminuka the great spirit of our lions, rivers, and caves never wanted this peculiar god who is inside their book. They tell us that in heaven we shall not labor. Why would a man long for that kind of happiness? Work is not suffering; it is not punishment for a man to do all he can for a good solid harvest. For a man not to labor is contemptible laziness. Shall we go to heaven to be lazy? To sit behind our huts and bask in the sun like lizards?

Scene 8: Holy Nehanda

Atmospheric music ushers in Nehanda.

NEHANDA: Who is this coming from the hills, from Chidamba, with her garments stained crimson?

CHAMINUKA AND NEHANDA: Who is this, robed in splendor, striding forward in the greatness of her eternity? *Nditaurire aniko!*

NEHANDA: I will not tell you that it is I, Nehanda the Spirit that battled wicked missionaries and criminal colonizers out of this here Zimbabwe, Zambia, Botswana, even before your grandfathers were boys.

I will not tell you that the white missionaries came and I said to my people, "Don't be afraid of them as they are only traders. Take a black cow to them and say this is the meat with which we greet you."

(Nehanda swallows hard.) But, why are these garments red, like those of one treading the winepress? Why are these garments red? *Nditaurire aniko!*

The blood of my children has *ngozi*; the blood of my children has unwanted spirits since mine was spilled. That *ngozi* will return to where it came from; it will return to the hands of the white missionary. Back to sender, back to sender.

(Tears well up in Nehanda's eyes.)

For they poured our blood on the ground, I will tell you this. *Ndichakutaurira.* My bones must rise again to avenge you. My bones will rise in the spirit of war. They will sing war songs with the harsh fire of battle. They will conjure new war songs and fight on until the shrines of the land of their birth are respected once more.

Scene 9: Epiphany/Let Them Eat Cake

Mama and Papa are getting ready for church, dressing in their colorful Sunday best. Mama places a cake on the table. It looks white from the outside because of the icing, but the cake itself is red, as we will find out. Mama has it out because she intends to give the cake to the homeless children at church.

MAMA: I am just saying that there is nothing sacred about our borders.

PAPA: You keep disturbing my ears with this idea. Anyhow, we have been at this talk of ancestors for hours.

(He notices the cake on the table.)

Is that the ruined cake you are going to give to the homeless children?

MAMA: Yes. Too much vanilla essence.

(She stares at the cake for a couple of beats and then quickly peeps through the curtain. She hears the sound of the neighbor's gate opening.)

Look at this silly woman next door basking in the sun like she owes me nothing. Since her party is finished, when is she going to return my pots? Actually, you know what? She can eat them.

PAPA: *(Deep sigh.)* So, how do you mean? About borders?

MAMA: *Ao!* Who drew them?

PAPA: Europeans, certainly.

MAMA: Why did they draw them?

PAPA: To organize our society. Do you not see how —

MAMA: No! When did you become dull? They were drawn up to serve European greed! They cut up this land between themselves like... like a cake!

(She begins to furiously gouge out hunks of the cake with her bare hands to illustrate this point. We see the redness of the cake.)

Take this piece, Belgium! *Ah merci bien.* Take this piece,

Britain! Long live the Queen. Here, Portugal! *Aluta bloody continua.* Here, France! Here, Germany! Here! Here!

(Her husband watches without speaking. Mama then grabs a white cotton swab to wipe her hands. The red of the cake looks bloody on her hands and on the cloth. In silence she puts the cloth away and, still in silence, snatches a piece of fried beef from the fridge.)

Ah, this maid! Even simple beef she cannot fry.

PAPA: Hmm... What a shame that we are headed for church. All these feelings you are having would go very well with chardonnay.

MAMA: Boemo makes sense, my husband. These countries are imaginary. The borders split apart ethnic groups and families. Even the word "tribe" is wrong, like Boemo said.

PAPA: Are you ready?

MAMA: *(Peeping through the curtain.)* This foolish woman says she cannot afford pots yet she can afford all this Brazilian hair to put on her head!

PAPA: Are you ready to leave for church, my wife?

MAMA: I should be able to claim the ancestral land our people roamed. Where are my earrings? Did you see my earrings, *rraabo?*

PAPA: Right there on the shelf.

MAMA: Thank you. Where is that boy? Let us go. We are going to miss church, *kana. Ei,* my husband, I cannot shake the feeling that the boy is right. These new ideas do not touch me right, but surely shared ancestors are more important than borders?

(Contemplatively.)

Should we even be worshiping in a congregational church?

PAPA: Let us not be radical, my wife.

MAMA: *(Aside.)* Hmm... I suppose that one does not tell a deaf person that war has broken out.

(Sincerely.) I do find these realizations uncomfortable, but they are very seductive ideas.

Where is he?

PAPA: Boemo! Boemo! Come downstairs, we are going.

Scene 10: 1985

BOEMO: I was born plump and healthy in 1985, the year that the first HIV/AIDS case was recorded in Botswana. I am of the first generation that has never experienced an HIV-free Botswana.

In 1985, other countries like Uganda had been battling AIDS for several years—fiercely, fearfully, and hopefully. Naturally we looked to Uganda for strategies on how to combat AIDS. Ugandans had successfully used music and theater arts like puppetry to inform the young and old and the infection rates were declining. We, too, wanted to use arts to sprinkle information everywhere on our native land.

Therefore, as I was growing up in Botswana, the only African languages of AIDS activism—both visually and musically—were Ugandan. Uganda's hero, activist-musician Philly Bongole Lutaaya became our hero in Botswana as well. Serious times had arrived and we lamented losses big and small. Ten-year-old children recited AIDS poems in school.

(Recites an AIDS poem, almost as an aside.)

you wreck us with your might/ you make pain rain in our eyes/ malome's sniffles before an open casket/ his son, a *lekolwane*, fine boy gone too soon/ what shall we call you? *pha-*

mo-kate! mogare! bolwetse!/ the sour yellow smell of hospital disinfectant for a hospital full of the infected/ shall we call you AIDS?

(Returns to the story of Philly Lutaaya.)

Just as AIDS has been a part of my Motswana experience, so has been Lutaaya's legacy, from five or six African countries away.

Scene 11: Philly Lutaaya

Philly begins to sing his Luganda hit song,"Diana." A cough stops him and after a long pause he speaks.

PHILLY LUTAAYA: *Gwe wange, era gwe gwenalonda. Nebwekiribakki no no, Sirikuleka. Kanjatule mu maaso ga bangi, Gwe wange era nze wuwo.*

Oba bwaavu, oba nno bwe bugagga. Nabeera nga naawe, kuba gwegwenalonda, Okufa kwe kulitwawula, gwe wange era nze wuwo.

Tuyambagane nga, Diana wulira olwalero, Lekka nkukuume, nga naawe Diana bwonkuuma, Nakulonda mubangi, Diana

babirye omulongo wo wo, Lekka nkutwaare maama ewange omutima gumbeere munteeko mwattu mweenya nze ndabbe akazigo, tambula ndabbe ebitumbwe, Simanyi nno bambi wotoli Diana ndibeera wa? Simanyi obiwulila Diana njazika ku matuugo, Akazigo mu manyo bwoseka mu oti mpulira nfiira wo,lekka nkutwaare mama ewange, nkakasa oja kweyagala.

(A coughing fit prevents Philly from finishing the song.)

I always tell myself: "Phillip, you may have traveled the world, but don't ever forget that you are African. You must be very proud of being African. Always, wherever you may go, identify yourself as a true African who knows that we are the sons and daughters of our grandfathers who labored for our glory and honor. Our dignity."

For the short time I have to live in this world, I want to lend a hand to fellow Ugandans who are fighting AIDS. I want to inform people. I will be the first prominent Ugandan, first African to declare that I have AIDS, to give AIDS a face.

(Pause.)

Furthermore, at this time, when our young Uganda nation is fighting to reconstruct herself, it needs all of us, including the sick and disabled. There must be no feeling of giving up. We must fight with all possible means to the last day. As a musician and writer, I regret that many songs, ideas, and sounds will never be heard. My work is nearly finished, but I promise that I will go on working with double the effort to see that I do all I can to serve you, Uganda. For me, there won't be any raising of the white flag to AIDS. The hunter in pursuit of an elephant does not stop to throw stones at birds; I will die fighting. For God and my country!

Scene 12: Itore Gape
("Re-dream Yourself" in Setswana)

Boemo is writing and thinking aloud...

BOEMO: I want to believe that a common ancestry is what binds us as Africans. I often imagine a common ancestor holding all Africans fiercely and warmly inside her womb. But we do not know that history, that womb. We are orphans. Bitter, broken, and beggarly orphans.

Our history of victories, intelligence, and organization has been successfully erased and replaced with sad fictions of—to borrow my dad's phrase—things tumbling into rough weather.

Years ago when I was a law student at Oxford, I met Africans from all over the continent. My three best friends were from Swaziland, Namibia, and Chad. It was sad, almost bitter, how little we knew of our common histories. Instead of history we bonded through common failures. We laughed at the spoils of the colonial attack. We ridiculed our cartoonish dictators covered in gold jewelry. We got drunk and painted pictures of our women who bleach their dark skin until it is orange. We imitated self-important and bureaucratic government employees.

(Laughs, almost maniacally.)

I believe it was Nietzsche who said, "Perhaps I know best why it is man alone who laughs; he alone suffers so deeply that he had to invent laughter."

Scene 13: The Way Things Should Be

Gulubani household. Mama just arrived home from work. Papa is already home.

MAMA: *Ei!* This heat. It has been curling around my neck all day. How was your day, my husband?

PAPA: Quite fine. I went to Parliament today and met with other MPs. We are trying to organize a petition to give us a salary increase.

MAMA: Let us hope it goes through this time.

PAPA: *(Kissing her on the cheek.)* How was yours, my wife?

MAMA: The usual. I had to refer a lot of people to the right offices. I never understood why everyone comes to us for inquiries. We are only the Office of the Ombudsman. We do not handle funerals for crying out loud.

PAPA: Funerals? What happened today?

MAMA: This man came in today just before tea break. I almost did not help him. Who comes just before tea break with many questions?

PAPA: So he wanted help with a funeral?

MAMA: Well, he wanted to bury a family member in a place that is not designated burial land. I told him to come back after lunch and he started talking about incompetence in the workplace. Then I pulled out my nail polish and ignored him. But he would not leave! He ranted and finally I told him *quickfastandinahurry* that before he can get burial space in that area, you have to fill out a pink form and sign your name in block capitals. You can get the form by first going through that door. You keep going straight, turn left and right and left again and there you will see a guard and you can ask him for office number 15, because our doors are not labeled. And then after that you take the body to the mortuary and come back next week. You have to make color photocopies of your *Omang* on 20 by 10 centimeters type of paper and take it to the police station to get them certified.

PAPA: Yes, of course. Why was he being a nincompoop? I tell you, things are all tumbling into rough weather.

(Pours two glasses of scotch. He hands one to his wife and takes a sip of his.)

MAMA: Well, that is not even the end of it. He started asking for the Director and I told him *quickfastandinahurry* that the Director is attending an international conference in Bangkok, Thailand. Then he asked for the Deputy Director and I told him that the Deputy Director is on sabbatical leave in the Okavango pondering the impact of HIV on the economy.

PAPA: Yes.

MAMA: But he went on to ask for the Minister himself! I was so annoyed that I could have burned those dreadlocks right off his foolish head! But being the Christian woman that I am, I still told him that the Minister is in Francistown as part of a working committee on how to manage youth with HIV/AIDS. I finally asked him what he wanted with those bosses that he could not tell me! At that moment I was almost twitching with annoyance. He wanted reimbursement for his deposit. Imagine! I told him point blank: our office does not deal with cases of reimbursement. You will need to talk to the mayor of Gaborone—go across the street!

PAPA: People do not know the respectful way things should be done anymore. It vexes me.

MAMA: Yes, me too!

(Takes a sip of her scotch.) Where is our son? Is he back from Parliament also?

PAPA: Yes. He is upstairs. I think he is drafting something. He is meeting with his constituents tomorrow. I am just pleased that he is working on something other than that bloody memoir.

MAMA: I say, the boy may be cantankerous with his ideas but he works hard for sure. My husband, you should talk to your people and make him a Cabinet Minister.

PAPA: We cannot rush a strategy, my wife. As my late father liked to say, "No strategy, no dynasty."

(He kisses her. They smile happily.)

Scene 14: All These People

BOEMO: I am formed of the Tswana people who ruled the land between the Okavango and the Vaal rivers. I am formed of the Kalangas ba-ka Nswazwi, of Mujaji the Rain Queen. I am formed of migrants who left Europe to find a new home on our native land. Whatever their own actions, they remain, part of me. In my veins courses the blood of the Malay slaves who came from the East. Their proud dignity informs my bearing, their culture a part of my essence. The stripes they bore on their bodies from the lash of the slave master are a reminder embossed on my consciousness of what should not be done.

Being part of all these people, and in the knowledge that none dare contest that assertion, I shall claim that I am an African and I am a Motswana.

I publish this memoir in honor of my loving parents, Zibanani and Cecilia Gulubani, who never knew that I could hear their drunken conversations about me from upstairs. I love you, Mom and Dad. And may you both rest in peace.

Botswana, re-imagine yourself.

THE END

GLOSSARY OF TERMS AND PHRASES

The selection of terms and phrases presented here are for the curious reader seeking more information about the local language and historical references found throughout both of Donald Molosi's plays. Since *Blue, Black and White* and *Motswana: Africa, Dream Again* are so closely related, the terms are combined into this single reference. Unless otherwise stated, the language is Setswana, a southern African language spoken by about five million people in Botswana, Namibia, South Africa, and Zimbabwe.

***

Akanya hela: Just imagine.

Ao!: An interjection expressing disbelief.

Ashanti or Asante: An ethnic group native to the Ashanti or Asante land of southern Ghana.

Bagaetsho: My people.

Bagammangwato ba ga mabiletsa: The title of a folksong that depicts the Bangwato people as rabble-rousers.

Bagolo bame ga ke dirise...: My elders I am not misusing...

Bagolo bame, lekgota le le hano: My elders, the *kgota* before me.

Bakwena: A Sotho-Tswana ethnic group in Botswana, Lesotho, and South Africa. Most of them have their totem as the crocodile.

Bangwaketse: An ethnic group in Botswana, most of whom reside in the environs of Kanye village in southeast Botswana. Most of them have their totem as the crocodile.

Bangwato: An ethnic group in Botswana hailing from Serowe village. Most of them have their totem as the duiker, a small antelope.

Barozwi: An ethnic group located mostly in southern Zimbabwe.

Basarwa: The indigenous people of the Kgalagadi (Kalahari) Desert, also found in Namibia and South Africa.

Batswana: The citizens of Botswana refer to themselves as Batswana (singular: Motswana).

Bechuanaland Protectorate: The name of the protectorate established in 1885 by the United Kingdom and Ireland in southern Africa. It became the Republic of Botswana in 1966.

Berbers: An indigenous ethnic group of nomadic people in northern Africa.

Bessie Head: Though she was born in South Africa, Head is considered Botswana's most important writer. Most of her important works are set in Serowe.

Boipuso: Independence.

Bokalaka: Land of the Kalangas, or where the Kalangas reside.

Bolwetse: Disease.

Cape: The southernmost point of South Africa where the Atlantic and Indian Oceans meet.

Chaminuka: This is the male counterpart of Nehanda. He is a spirit believed to have powers of bringing rain and controlling animals.

Chidamba: A range of hills in central Zimbabwe.

Chinoyi: A group of caves in northern Zimbabwe. They were named after a chief who used them as refuge from Ndebele raiders in the 19th century.

Chobe: A national park in northern Botswana containing one of the biggest concentrations of wildlife in Botswana.

"Diana": A love song by Philly Lutaaya. Some of the lyrics: You are mine and I am yours. We will be together in prosperity and in poverty. Turn around and let me see your calf muscles [a sign of beauty in Buganda, Uganda]. Smile, let me see the gap between your teeth [another sign of beauty]. (For the curious, the song is easily found with a search on YouTube.)

Dimawe: The location of the Battle of Dimawe (August 1852), led by Kgosi Sechele. The battle involved several Batswana tribes defending—successfully—Dimawe Hill from the Boers.

Dranksberg: The largest escarpment in southern Africa, located in Lesotho.

Dumelang: Hello.

E le gore: To be clear.

Edison Masisi (1921–2003): Masisi was a Botswanan politician and diplomat. He served as the second foreign minister from 1969–1971.

El Negro Banyoles, the Mothaping King: An African man whose body was exhumed in 1829, eviscerated to be exhibited at first in France and then the Darder Museum of Natural History in Banyoles, Spain. His remains were repatriated to Botswana in 2001 for burial at Tsholofelo Park.

Francistown: Botswana's second largest city.

Ga ke re…: Isn't it true that…

Gatwe o ne a na le watch mo pelong!: It is said that he had a watch in his heart!

Gcwihaba: An underground labyrinth of caverns and pits, linked passages, and stalagmite and stalactite formations in northern Botswana.

Gulubani: A village in the Kalanga area (northeast) of Botswana.

Hei, hei wee: An interjection that acts as a placeholder for a word. It is like the English "blah-blah." It mimics speech.

Hottentot Venus: See Saartjie Baartman.

Ian Khama: Son of Botswana's founding president, Sir Seretse Khama. Ian Khama is the current president of Botswana and has been in office since 2008.

Ija (also Ijaa; Ijo): An interjection in speech to express disapproval and embarrassment.

Juba: The capital city of South Sudan, the newest African country.

Ka jalo ke ne ke kopa gore le mo amogele ka mabogo oo mabe-di...: So I was begging to openly welcome...

Kalanga: One of the oldest of the Shona ethnic groups. The Kalangas are along the Botswana-Zimbabwe border; they are ethnic minorities in both countries.

Kalangas ba-ka Nswazi: Originally a Sotho-Tswana group that assimilated into the larger Kalanga ethnic group.

Kana: By the way.

Ke a go rata: I love you.

Ke a itse: I know.

Ke le ngwana wa gago...: As your child...

Ke ne ke sale todise matho bagolo mme ha le eletsa keka le rereisa gape ka ngwetsi ya lona: I was not overlooking you my elders, but if you want I will re-introduce your daughter-in-law...

Kenneth Kaunda: Zambia's founding president, who was in office from 1964 to 1991. His greatest legacy is his role in the Zambian struggle for independence from British rule.

Kgalagadi: A desert in the southwest of Botswana, bordering Namibia. Also known as the Kalahari.

Kgosi Khama the Great III: He was the King of the Bangwato people from 1837 to 1923.

Kgosi Moshoeshoe: King of Basotho, from 1822 to 1870. He is known for his donation of land to protect refugees from neighboring kingdoms.

Kgosi Sechele I: He was the King of the Bakwena (one of the major Tswana ethnic groups). Sechele I led the Kwena people at the Battle of Dimawe in 1852, where they defeated the South Africans and retained their land.

Kgota: 1. A village ward. 2. A place where the village leaders convene.

Khoi (Khoisan): A collective name for the hunter-gatherer indigenous people of southern Africa. Also called San.

King Shaka Zulu (Nkosi Shaka Zulu): The king of the Zulu nation from 1816 to 1828. He is known to have united the northern Nguni people.

Lekolwane: A well-groomed young man.

Linyanti: A river at the corner of the Chobe National Park. Part of this river is also in Namibia.

Makgadikgadi: A group of salt pans in northeast Botswana.

Malay slaves: People of Malay origin whom in the 15th century were kidnapped and forced into slavery by European settlers in South Africa.

Malome: Maternal uncle.

Maphiri: The name of Seretse Khama's ancestors on his mother's side.

Matebele: Setswana for a Zimbabwean ethnic group.

Mbuya Nehanda: The spirit medium/leader for the Zezuru and Shona people. Her spirit is believed to be an ancestral spirit, that of a lion, and is responsible for guiding Zimbabwean soldiers to victory in the Chimurenga War of 1896-7. The spirit of Nehanda is always accompanied by its male counterpart, Chaminuka.

Miriam Makeba: Makeba was a South African singer and civil rights activist. In the 1960s she popularized African music around the world.

Mmaabo: Mother of (my/the) children.

Mmegi: The name of a Botswana daily newspaper.

Mogare: Virus.

Mohumagadi: Queen.

Moratiwa: Beloved.

Morwa Kgosi: Prince. The literal translation is "son of a king."

Mothaping or Motlhaping: One belonging to the Thaping or Tlhaping ethnic group. They are a Tswana ethnic group and are found in Botswana and South Africa.

Motsamai Mpho: A political figure who was a member of the African National Congress (ANC) and later founded the Botswana People's Party (BPP). He is said to have named the Republic of Botswana.

Motswana: The singular of Batswana, which is how the people of Botswana refer to themselves.

Mudzimu: Shona for "ancestral spirit."

Mujaji the Rain Queen: Queen of the Balobedu (17th and 18th century) in the Limpopo province of South Africa, believed to have had special powers to control the clouds and rainfall.

Her royal lineage is one of the few matrilineal ones in Southern Africa.

Mxm!: Interjection. A disapproving sucking of the teeth. Very common.

Ndebele: People of southwestern Zimbabwe who now live primarily around the city of Bulawayo.

Ndichakutaurira: Shona for "I will tell you."

Nditaurire aniko: Shona for "I will not tell anyone."

Ndokuda: Kalanga for "I love you."

Ne betshoo: Betsho means "my people," just like "bagaetsho." The "ne" implies a question.

Nehanda: See Mbuya Nehanda.

Ngozi: Shona for "bad spirit."

Ngwanaka: My child.

Ngwato: The largest Tswana ethnic group in Botswana, mainly located in the central part of the country. Their royal base is Serowe village. "Ngwato" is also a suffix indicating something that pertains to Bangwato.

Nkange: A region in northern Botswana, occupied mainly by the Kalanga.

Nswazwi, King of the Kalangas: Nswazwi was a king of the Kalanga people, one of Botswana's largest minority groups (who also have a presence in Zimbabwe).

Nutford House: Built in 1916 and acquired by the University of London in 1949.

Okavango: A delta in Botswana that covers more than 1,600 km^2.

Omang: Botswana's identity card.

Ota Benga: A Congolese man, a pygmy, who was freed from African slave traders to be exhibited in various places in the U.S. He eventually committed suicide from the frustration of being exhibited and forcibly exiled from his native land.

Pasipamire: He was believed to be the spirit medium of Chaminuka in the late 19th century.

Phamo-kate!: Onomatopoeic moniker for AIDS. *Phamo* is onomatopoeic for the act of grabbing and *kate!* is onomatopoeic for burying something.

Philly Bongole Lutaaya (1951-89): A Ugandan musician and the first prominent African to give a human face to the HIV/AIDS crisis by publicly declaring his positivity in 1988.

Pula: Rain. Water is a prized commodity in Botswana's semi-arid climate, and so rain is seen as a blessing.

Ra re: We are saying.

Rampholo Molefhe: A veteran columnist and journalist who was especially prolific in the new Republic of Botswana.

Rhodesia: The British South Africa Company of Cecil Rhodes first demarcated the territory in the 1890s; it became the self-governing British colony of Southern Rhodesia in 1923. Today it's known as Zimbabwe.

Rraabo: Father of (my/the) children.

Rrangwane: Paternal uncle.

Russ Molosiwa: A veteran journalist in Botswana and contemporary of Rampholo Molefhe.

Ruth Williams: Williams (1923-2002) was the white British wife of Botswana's founding President Sir Seretse Khama.

Saartjie Baartman: A Khoikhoi woman who was trafficked to Europe in the 19th century to be exhibited for what Europeans found to be unusually large buttocks.

San: See Khoi.

Sekgoma: The father of Seretse Khama.

Sekuru Kaguvi: A leader in the Shona rebellion during the first Chimurenga (revolutionary struggle; 1896-7) whose body was inhabited by the spirit Chaminuka.

Serowe: The largest village in Botswana. It is the royal capital of the Bangwato ethnic group.

Shania Twain: A Canadian singer-songwriter of country pop.

Shona: The largest ethnic group in Zimbabwe. Historically, the Shona came to being out of an amalgamation of other southern African ethnic groups.

Sophiatown: A Black cultural hub in South Africa that was destroyed under apartheid in the 1940s and 1950s. It was then built back as Triomf, then in 2006 it returned to its original name.

South African Maburu: Maburu is another term for the Boers.

Struizendam: A village in the Kgalagadi District of Botswana. Struizendam is the most southern village of its size in Botswana and barely receives any rain throughout the year due to desert conditions.

Suka lapha!: Xhosa for "get out of here."

Swahili: An ethnic and linguistic group in the African Great Lakes region and East Africa.

Tanganyika: Tanganyika was a sovereign state from 1961 to 1964, situated between the Indian Ocean and the African Great

Lakes of Victoria, Nyasa, and Tanganyika. The territory has been absorbed into present day Tanzania.

Tshekedi Khama: The regent of the Bangwato ethnic group in 1923 after the death of Sekgoma II. He is also Seretse Khama's uncle.

Tswana: A southern African ethnic group, mostly in South Africa and Botswana. Ironically when African countries were demarcated in 1852, there were more Tswana people in South Africa than in Botswana.

Tswapong Hills: A group of hills in eastern Botswana, host to numerous archaeological, historical, and natural history sites.

Vaal: A tributary of the Orange River in South Africa. Historically, the river formed the border between the Basotho Kingdom and the Union of South Africa.

Waitse wena!: As for you!

Xhosa: One of the major southern African ethnic groups. Xhosas mostly live in the southeastern part of South Africa.

Zambezi: The fourth-longest river in Africa. It runs through nine countries: Angola, Botswana, Democratic Republic of Congo, Malawi, Mozambique, Namibia, Tanzania, Zambia, and Zimbabwe.

ABOUT DONALD MOLOSI

Donald Molosi is a classically-trained actor and award-winning playwright. He holds an MA in Performance Studies from UCSB, a Graduate Diploma in Classical Acting from LAMDA, and a BA in Political Science and Theatre from Williams College.

Molosi is featured in *A United Kingdom*, opposite Golden Globe and Emmy award nominee David Oyelowo and Oscar nominee Rosamund Pike. The film depicts the marriage of Prince Seretse Khama and Ruth Williams in the 1940s and the uniting of the people of Botswana.

Molosi divides his time between Botswana and the United States.

ABOUT THE MANTLE

The Mantle publishes emerging critics, writers, and intellectuals in the arts, international affairs, literature, and philosophy. We foster discourse with a global audience through critiques, essays, fiction, and interviews. We pay close attention to voices with limited exposure in their home countries and the English language, as well as individuals experiencing censorship. Read essays on our online magazine at www.mantlethought.org and explore our print and ebook titles at www.mantlebooks.com.